The New Junior Worlers Manual

A Text - Book On Junior Work

by

Rev. Robert P. Anderson

Editorial Secretary of the
United Society of
Christian Endeavor

First Fruits Press
Wilmore, Kentucky
c2015

The new junior workers' manual: a text-book on junior work, by Rev. Robert P. Anderson.

First Fruits Press, ©2015
Previously published: Boston, Chicago : United Society of Christian Endeavor ©1921.

ISBN: 9781621714118 (print), 9781621714125 (digital)

Digital version at http://place.asburyseminary.edu/christianendeavorbooks/4/

First Fruits Press is a digital imprint of the Asbury Theological Seminary, B.L. Fisher Library. Asbury Theological Seminary is the legal owner of the material previously published by the Pentecostal Publishing Co. and reserves the right to release new editions of this material as well as new material produced by Asbury Theological Seminary. Its publications are available for noncommercial and educational uses, such as research, teaching and private study. First Fruits Press has licensed the digital version of this work under the Creative Commons Attribution Noncommercial 3.0 United States License. To view a copy of this license, visit http://creativecommons.org/licenses/by-nc/3.0/us/.

For all other uses, contact:

First Fruits Press
B.L. Fisher Library
Asbury Theological Seminary
204 N. Lexington Ave.
Wilmore, KY 40390
http://place.asburyseminary.edu/firstfruits

Anderson, Robert Phillips, 1866-
    The new junior workers' manual : a text-book on junior work / by Rev. Robert P. Anderson.
    187 pages ; 21 cm.
    Wilmore, Ky. : First Fruits Press, ©2015.
    Reprint. Previously published: Boston : United Society of Christian Endeavor, ©1921.
    ISBN: 9781621714118 (pbk.)
    1. United Society of Christian Endeavor. I. Title.
BV1429 .A6 2015

Cover design by Jonathan Ramsay

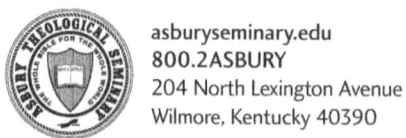

asburyseminary.edu
800.2ASBURY
204 North Lexington Avenue
Wilmore, Kentucky 40390

First Fruits Press
The Academic Open Press of Asbury Theological Seminary
204 N. Lexington Ave., Wilmore, KY 40390
859-858-2236
first.fruits@asburyseminary.edu
asbury.to/firstfruits

The New Junior Workers' Manual

A TEXT-BOOK ON JUNIOR WORK

BY

Rev. Robert P. Anderson

Editorial Secretary of the United
Society of Christian Endeavor

UNITED SOCIETY OF CHRISTIAN ENDEAVOR
BOSTON : : CHICAGO

Copyrighted, 1921

by the

UNITED SOCIETY OF CHRISTIAN ENDEAVOR

CONTENTS

CHAPTER	PAGE
I. WHY?	11
The Aim of Junior Endeavor	12
Why a Junior Society Is Needed	13
What about a Superintendent for the Juniors?	13
How Should a Junior Superintendent Be Appointed?	15
II. THE CHILD	17
The Child's Thought	18
Early Childhood	19
The Junior Age	20
The Body	22
The Mind	24
The Child's Interests	27
Thought, Feeling, and Will	28
Instinct	30
Habit	36
III. MORALS AND RELIGION	41
Education of the Moral Life	41
What Morality Means to Children	42
The Lying Habit	43
Child Virtues	44
The Child's Religion	45
IV. THE SUPERINTENDENT'S TASK	49
General Principles	50
Discipline	54
Restless Juniors	56
What to Teach	59

CONTENTS

CHAPTER	PAGE
V. QUALIFICATIONS OF THE SUPERINTENDENT	63
Love	63
Personality	64
Patience	64
Justice	65
Consecration	65
Tact	66
Knowledge	66
Pastor Superintendents	66
VI. ORGANIZATION AND EQUIPMENT	68
How to Organize a Junior Society	68
Two Methods	69
The Assistants	71
The Membership	72
The Active Members' Pledge	72
The Preparatory Members' Pledge	73
The Constitution	74
The Equipment	79
Society Equipment	80
VII. THE OFFICERS	83
The President	83
The Vice-President	83
The Secretary	84
The Treasurer	85
Executive-Committee Meeting	88
The Society's Business Meeting	89
VIII. SOCIETY ORGANIZATION: THE COMMITTEES	91
Prayer-Meeting Committee	92
Lookout Committee	93
Social Committee	97
Recreation Committee	100
Missionary Committee	101

CONTENTS

CHAPTER		PAGE
	Sunshine Committee	104
	Flower Committee	105
	Birthday Committee	106
	Good-Citizenship Committee	106
	Scrap-Book Committee	107
	Music Committee	108
	Information Committee	108
	Good-Literature Committee	109
IX.	HOW TO CONDUCT A JUNIOR MEETING	111
	The Time of Meeting	111
	The Programme	113
	Pageants	119
	Repetition and Enforcement	119
	The Consecration Meeting	121
X.	WHAT THE SOCIETY MAY DO	123
XI.	JUNIOR EDUCATIONAL PROGRAMME	131
	1. The Body	131
	2. The Mind	131
	A. Thought	132
	B. Feeling	132
	C. Will	133
	3. The Soul	133
	Missionary Education	134
	Co-ordinate the Work	134
	The Child's Quiet Hour	136
	The Tenth Legion	138
	A Society Educational Policy	140
XII.	BIBLE DRILLS AND MEMORY WORK	147
	A. BIBLE DRILLS	147
	Learning the Names of the Bible Books	147
	Verse-Finding Drill	151

CONTENTS

CHAPTER	PAGE

    Spelling Drill 152
    Combination Drill and Memory Work...... 152
    A Parable Drill 153
    Map Drills 153
    Bible Biography Drill 154
  B. BIBLE ALPHABETS 155
    A Great-Word Alphabet.................. 155
    Other Alphabets 157
    "I Am" Verses 158
    "I Will" or Words of Invitation......... 158
    More "I Will" Verses 159
    Symbols of the Spirit Verses............. 159
    Memory Work in Connection with Great
      Topics 160
    God's Gifts 160
    Practical Passages: Old Testament........ 161
    Practical Passages: New Testament....... 161
    A Bible Biography Alphabet.............. 162
  Rewards 165

XIII. SHORT BIBLE PRAYERS...................... 167
  Supplication 167
  Aspiration 168
  Praise 169
  Faith 170
  Thanksgiving 170
  Dedication 171
  Benedictions 171
  Using the Bible in Prayer................. 173
  Some Sentence Prayers 174

XIV. A FEW SUGGESTIONS 176
  Sashes, Stars, Crescents, and Suns........ 176
  Parents and the Pledge.................... 177

CONTENTS

CHAPTER PAGE

    Mothers' Meetings 177
    Banners 178
    Buttons and Pins 180

XV. JUNIOR UNIONS 181
    The Superintendents 181
    Round Robins 182
    The Junior Union 182
    The Junior Parade 184
    Automobile Parade 185
    The Junior Union Treasury................. 185
    The Junior Union Secretary................ 186

The New Junior Workers' Manual

CHAPTER I

WHY?

The Junior society is no longer an experiment. It has stood the test of time and experience. This handbook, therefore, is not a defence of Junior work, but an attempt to present to superintendents some principles and methods that may help them in their labors.

The Junior society does one very definite service for the child. It more than doubles the time given to its religious instruction. The Sunday-school hour is all too short for the task. The Junior society adds another hour, and to this again whatever time is devoted during the week to committee work. The effect of this extra training, especially in view of the character of it, is to give a distinct advantage to the child that passes through the society.

Some Sunday-schools have adopted the Junior society's system of memory work and drills and are getting good results. But the time that can be given to this work in a Sunday school is very limited, if the school is to carry out its instructional features well. And of course there is a multitude of schools in which memory work is either of the scantiest or is altogether lacking. Junior training supplements the Sunday school at this point to a marked degree. Many adults who for the first time see a Junior society in operation are astounded at the efficiency of the Juniors in finding Bible verses anywhere in the Bible, and at the extent of their Bible knowledge.

The Aim of Junior Endeavor.—The aim of Junior Endeavor is Christian nurture, to increase the children's knowledge of the Bible, teach them how to use the Book, establish desirable habits in the habit-forming age, set up worthy ideals in the period of greatest openness to suggestion and greatest tendency to imitation, arouse and educate conscience, lead them to accept Christ as Saviour and Lord, and to apply to the need and capacity of children the principle of the older society, to learn by doing. The society is fundamentally not an attempt to do something for the child, but rather to get the child to do something for himself. The aim is not to make children grown up before their time, but to give them an opportunity to practise in childhood's way what they can of Christianity.

Why a Junior Society Is Needed.—It is needed because Juniors are given more and better religious education with it than without it. It is needed because it provides expressional work, or teaching by doing, for which there is not time in the Sunday school. It is needed because it ministers to instincts that are especially strong in the Junior age. It helps to develop a spirit of reverence and worship. It lays the foundation of a good conscience in after years. It teaches children that they have responsibilites and duties. It trains them to pray, to testify, and it is a splendid and altogether necessary preparation for the work of the Intermediate and Senior societies.

Again, in the society Juniors are drawn close to the superintendent and naturally imitate her ideals, thus establishing good habits that set as the years move on. The power of a consecrated personality on a child's mind is great beyond words. What a superintendent can do in the way of teaching is excellent, but what she can do by the influence of her character and personality is more wonderful still.

What about a Superintendent for the Juniors?—If Junior work were really understood there would be no difficulty in finding a superintendent for the society. No opportunity for service that the church supplies is greater than that of guiding a group of Juniors. The children are at the most impressionable age. Their minds are plastic, ready to take whatever stamp is placed upon them. These years are vital, often determining the entire life. Surely there are in the church or the Senior society one or two young people with vision and understanding and consecration who will hear Christ's call not only to follow Him but also to feed His lambs! Those that sigh for the privilege of service on the foreign field (and there are many in our societies) should look at the children at their very doors, a field quite as important and far more fruitful than the field in any country across the sea. The children of the church are often overlooked, the idea being that the Sunday school is fully taking care of them. Plenty of churches pay more for a quartette or a soloist to enrich the Sunday services than they would think of paying for the equipment and support of a Junior society. Some churches are indeed alive to their opportunity and are employing paid workers for their children. That is beyond the ability of most, however, so that the Junior superintendent will generally be a voluntary worker.

We shall have more to say later about the qualifications of the Junior superintendent. At present it is enough to point out that any young man or young woman of ordinary intelligence can fit himself or herself for the work.

The church should have some means of training superintendents for the Junior society. At present the usual way one can get training is by serving as assistant superintendent under a wide-awake leader. Every society should have at least one assistant superintendent; two or more are better. In this way understudies are ready to take up the work if the superintendent should move away or be unable to continue it. But even where there is no society a young person need not be afraid to take hold. A grasp of fundamental principles is not difficult for an Endeavorer who already has experience in the older society, and there is abundant literature on Junior work. The helps for the topic in *The Junior Christian Endeavor World* and in *The Christian Endeavor World* are enough to ensure a good meeting.

How Should the Junior Superintendent Be Appointed?—There is really no rule. In some cases the church, through its official board, appoints. In other cases the Senior Christian Endeavor society appoints not only a superintendent but several assistants, or what is called a Junior committee. In other cases there is no appointment at all; a consecrated young woman sees the need and asks the pastor for permission to form a society. Again, sometimes the women's organizations in the church appoint a superintendent for the Juniors. The important thing is that some one takes up the work. If we were asked to give our preference as to method, we would say that perhaps the appointment of a superintendent through the official board of the church is the best plan. It gives official standing to the society. But even in that case the superintendent would have to be found first. One point seems important, namely, that the superintendent chosen shall be or shall have been an Endeavorer. The Junior society will be conducted along the same general lines as the Senior society, with suitable modifications, and one that has had Christian Endeavor training will know fairly well what should be done. If there is no one in the church who has had this training, then do the next best thing and appoint one who is willing to learn.

QUESTIONS FOR REVIEW

What service does Junior Christian Endeavor do for the child?
How does Junior Christian Endeavor supplement the Sunday school?
What is the aim of Junior Endeavor?
Why is a Junior society needed?
Why should young people be willing to become Junior superintendents?
How may a Junior superintendent get training?
How should a Junior superintendent be appointed?

CHAPTER II

THE CHILD

The Junior superintendent will love children. This is essential. But she ought also to understand children. She should have *insight* into their mode of acting and thinking. This is necessary if she is to teach them efficiently and to maintain discipline. This is the problem before us now.

The Junior age is from about seven to thirteen or fourteen. How do Juniors of this age think and act? We must remember that childhood is very complex and that children are different from one another, just like grown-ups. Few boys and girls fit exactly into any formula. Therefore we must watch the individual, keep our eyes and ears open for signs of what the child is thinking, and seek to find a motive for his acts; we must study the nature of the child and how to approach him, how to influence him for good, how to establish right habits and combat wrong ones, how to give the child a conception of God, of Christ, of the Bible, of the Christian life. This is no mean task, but it is one which, rightly carried through, pays rich dividends in the lives of boys and girls.

The Child's Thought.—We must try to realize at all times that the child thinks differently from a grown person. This is natural, for a child's experience is exceedingly limited. Most situations he has to face are new to him. He has been born into a bewildering world which he does not in the least understand, but about which he is tremendously curious. He wants to try everything and feel the effect of what he does. He is hungry for experiences of all sorts.

A grown person, that is, a person who has enriched his experience in the course of time, will have acquired through this experience a whole collection of ideals and motives which the child has not at all. In a given situation, therefore, a grown person will act from a more or less definite set of motives that lie at the back of his mind. But the child has no experience to guide him in a strange situation. He acts as we say impulsively; that is, he tries out a course of action that seems right to him in the circumstances, a course that is really hit or miss and not carefully reasoned or thought through. He cannot think a thing through because he has not the material for thought to work upon.

The younger a child is the more likely he is to react differently from older persons to the various situations in which he finds himself. The superintendent should remember this. She should never judge a child by her own standard either of intelligence or morals, but seek in every instance to get the point of view of the child. She must put herself in his place. Only as this is grasped, or as the superintendent has *insight* and understanding, will she be able to exert her full influence on the child. For the education of children does not merely consist in pouring information into empty brains, or making the little folks memorize facts, but in developing their mental and spiritual powers. In reality children educate themselves; the most that we can do is to furnish them with the material and the opportunity, and guide their efforts as they seek to touch reality.

Early Childhood.—This is not the place to discuss the mental processes of early childhood. In the first six years the child's activity is predominantly muscular. The physical senses are being trained, and the child is getting more and more control of its body. This does not mean that there is no mental or spiritual activity during these years, or that full control of the body is gained at the early age of six, but simply that there is more muscular than any other kind of activity in this period, the mental and spiritual being secondary. Perhaps this is not an exact statement, for there is really nothing secondary in a child's growth. All growth goes on at the same time, but not at the same rate. In the early days physical growth outstrips mental and spiritual.

The Junior Age.—As we have said, in relation to the Junior society the Junior age is from seven to thirteen or fourteen. This does not mean that in this entire period the mental condition of children is the same. It is not. The years from seven to ten are different in many ways from those between ten and thirteen. Still, there is no abrupt change in a child's development. Growth is gradual, and if anything seems abrupt to us, we may be sure that there has been a long period of silent preparation for the change. A flower may unfold in a day, but the bud is the work of an extended period.

In both of these ages, seven—ten, ten—thirteen, many characteristics and instincts are similar, but the older Juniors are not only enlarging their experience and deepening their emotional life, but are developing their reasoning powers, and in these ways are adding new characteristics or changing the emphasis on the old. A work on psychology would probably attempt to draw a different picture for each age; for our purpose it will be enough to describe in general the characteristics and interests of the entire period, noting as we go along those traits that are modified or expanded by growing experience and reason.

THE CHILD 21

The fact is that the characteristics of early childhood live on through all the Junior years, modified in various ways. Early childhood, or the years from one to six or seven, is the play period. The child thinks of his activities. His environment, the strange world about him, awakens his curiosity, and his little head is full of questions. He is hungering for experience. He tries to reproduce in his own life the things he sees around him. He is imitative. He plays games taken from life or from stories he has heard; he is soldier, hunter, preacher, knight, engineer, and so forth. Girls are wrapped up in their dolls, reproducing adult life. It is this hunger for experience, unrestrained by reason, that gives the child what is called the roving disposition. He has no thought of danger as he wanders away. It never occurs to him that he is doing wrong or causing anxiety and pain. Thought is uncontrolled and is immediately translated into action. He thinks of walking off, and away he goes. To think is to do; impulse rules, without consideration of effects. Indeed a child does not at this age *reason* from cause to effect at all. His experience will gradually teach him this truth, as when a hot stove burns his fingers. He will recall later, when tempted to touch another hot stove, what happened the last time he did this. Repeated incidents of this kind cause him to reflect. Life is admirably suited to awaken the reasoning faculty, and experience is one of its methods.

In early childhood, then, we find the roots of many traits that develop later. Take the collecting instinct which in more mature life becomes a hobby or a science. Before seven it manifests itself in a crude way. Examine a boy's pockets and see what they contain—nails, string, a top, a piece of wire, spools, and so on. There is a dim impulse to annex things (the roots, perhaps, of the rights of property), but everything is very crude, for the mental activity of the period is narrow.

The Body.—The growth of the body is accompanied by great physical activity or play. Running games are in favor. With growing control over his muscles and with increasing intelligence, the child begins to take pride in his skill. His thought is concentrated on what he is doing. He is a thoroughgoing individualist. Team play is beyond him—he cannot yet put himself into the place of the other fellow. He cannot see why he should subordinate himself for the good of the team or the winning of a game. He wants to win, of course, but the emphasis is on himself; *he* wants to win. Group games do not therefore make the same appeal to young children as games which call forth the full powers of each player on his or her own behalf.

Physical activity, skill, individualism are accompanied by a growing apprehension of *ends*. The acts of the child become purposeful as reason begins to come into his own. The child is still impulsive, but we see checks rising in the mind that tend to call a halt, and there is a more or less clear choice of purposes and more tenacity in holding to a course once decided upon. A young child can easily be coaxed to give up a purpose or relinquish a desire simply by placing a new object of desire before him. But in later childhood this is more difficult. The child knows what he wants.

Imitation, already seen in early childhood, grows more effective after the age of seven. The child still plays games taken from grown-up life. He is in reality trying to experience such life as he sees around him, trying to get the "feel" of it, trying it on himself as one might try on a suit of clothes. Thus the child will play house or school, or act as policeman, fireman, preacher, engineer, farmer, tramp, according to his experience and in order that he may *be* these people. He really desires to *be* the persons he imitates; for the time being they are his heroes. With great frankness boys or girls will tell you what they want to be in life; own a candy store (evidently that they may eat all the candy they please), be policemen, showmen, bareback riders, cowboys, soldiers, seamen, and so forth. Probably fifty out of every hundred girls have at some time wished to be milliners or dressmakers. If you discuss the matter with them they will reason out their preference, and the reasons will seem cogent to them, however childish they appear to adult intelligence.

In connection with imitation it should be said that these years are years of great suggestibility. The child is liable to do the thing he sees or that is suggested to him. And suggestion is made not only in words but in pictures, in books, in shows, in entertainments. The mind is plastic; the emotions rule; so that almost anything that will touch a child's interest can be deeply impressed on his nature. This fact is one that the Junior superintendent should never forget. Everything that happens before the eyes of a child is a suggestion and will produce some effect upon his character, good or bad, according to the nature of the thing.

The Mind.—Imitation, of course, is a mental trait although it issues in physical activity. The powers of the mind grow apace. After seven curiosity is quite as keen as before. Questions are freely asked, but with growing intelligence. Memory is at its best. The perceptions that have come through the senses have become assimilated and grouped and arranged. Memory labels and can recall all sorts of experiences. Memory is simply the retention of impressions and ideas, which includes the power to recall them when wanted.

Imagination is the combining of ideas and impressions so that new ideas arise out of them. At this age memory and imagination are active, as we have said, trying on life, reaching out like an eager hand for more. Imagination will grow deeper and richer later in life, but memory will never be better than in the Junior years from seven to thirteen.

The crude collections of childhood give place now to more elaborate ones. Desire is strong—for desire is at the very bottom of life itself—and it is not always properly controlled by reason and experience. Desire is personal, of course; that is, what a child desires he desires *for himself*, and this makes for individualism. The interests of the child are always self-centred. The world has one centre—himself. The importance of things is judged by the way in which they affect him. He will grow out of this in time; but it is essential that we understand how he looks upon things until he learns better or is taught different.

The Junior is gaining skill and he will show more attention now to the details of the things he makes. His will is gaining in forcefulness, and sometimes the lack of experience combined with vigorous will power look to us almost like obstinacy. Susceptibility to impressions is very great, and many a life is destroyed from this cause at this early age.

The key to the understanding of childhood is the realization of the child's position and his lack of mental equipment. It would be very easy to overemphasize the difference between children and grown persons. There is a difference, of course, which must be kept in mind, but it is the difference between immaturity and experience. The variations are on the surface and are non-essential; the similarities are in the depths and are fundamental. All the capacities of a grown person's mind are potential in the child. It is true that the brain of a child is smaller than that of a man; but it is made of the same stuff. It is true that a man's experience is much larger than that of a child, but every day is bringing the child closer to the man in this respect. He has in an immature state all the capacities of manhood and maturity. He has thought, feeling, and will. The child's mind works under the same laws of association as a man's mind. If it were essentially different from the mind of an adult we could not hope to understand it at all.

Suppose we were introduced to a new planet, Mars, let us say, where life and emotion and intellect are enormously more mature than anything we have ever known on earth. We should be forced to reconstruct all our thinking and feeling if we were to fit ourselves to that new life. We should surely hunger for those experiences that yet lay outside of our knowledge, and we should doubtless make mistakes and appear to the Martians as very childish beings if we had nothing to guide us in the selection of our courses except our narrow experience, and had not the sense to trust wise leadership. That is the position of the child. It is in a new world and is as yet a stranger.

The Child's Interests.—Some one has said that the art of education is that of appealing to the child's interests and guiding them aright.

Now, as we have seen, the early interests of the child are mostly physical and active, and these interests remain throughout childhood. There is the play interest, very wide and very important, which indeed has a physical basis, but has mental and moral values as well. Play includes imitation, as in all sorts of games and handwork; for desire is strong to make things, to handle and win mastery over all kinds of material. These interests are good for health; they develop the muscles, giving necessary control over the body, and they also develop skill in all tasks. The child does not live in a group of separate compartments, with play in one, memory in another, and so on, but is a growing *person* and must be studied in terms of personality. Physical activity therefore cannot be physical alone, for it has an effect on the mind and the heart; it teaches the child to think and to feel. There is no better way to educate the child in some directions than through the instinct to play.

Mental interests are seen in curiosity, in ability to take pains in working out details, in reasoned purposes, in the joy that comes from memorizing, in attaining knowledge, in entering into the experience of others, in making collections, and so on.

Thought, Feeling; and Will.—An analysis of mental processes reveals three phases of mental activity, thought, feeling, and will. This division is helpful, but we must not imagine that there is an essential difference between these three processes. They are never utterly separated. There never was thought which had no tinge of feeling, or feeling that had no tinge of thought, at least in human beings. The self or the ego is central; it is the self that thinks, that feels, that wills, and sometimes it does all three at once. Feeling is only an aspect of thought. So is will. If there were no thought there could be neither feeling nor will; and there would be nothing at all without the central ego, the person who experiences all three.

Thought is that mental process which results in knowledge. It is primarily fed by the senses: sight, touch, hearing, taste, smell. Through these channels the outer world enters into the ego and makes an impression on the person, and intellect interprets that impression. It detects a meaning in it. In its simplest form knowledge is the interpretation of sensation. This is the foundation even of the highest kind of knowledge.

On the other hand feeling has to do with the pleasure or pain that result from experience or impressions. The color of a rose, or the smell of a flower may produce a thrill of feeling or of pleasure; the sight of ugliness or of an accident will produce a feeling of pain. Who does not know the pang of disappointment? Who has not experienced the thrill of beautiful music? A good deal of our thinking, if we were to analyze it, would be found to be colored by our emotions.

Will is not something distinct from thought. It is thought that arrives at a decision. The mind is not merely a mirror that receives in its depths every image presented before it. It is not passive. It is moved to intense activity by impressions made upon it. The entering thought is like a chemical thrown into a crucible that already contains other chemicals. Not only do the contents of the mind rise to welcome or reject a newcomer, but the ego also takes a hand. Of course the ego may be prejudiced by the presence of many other thoughts that it has made welcome before. But prejudiced or not, it acts. This action of the mind is termed will. The outgoing response to the incoming impression is will. In common speech, when the mind determines to act, this determination is called an act of will.

Now the child has thought, as yet immature and narrow; and feeling, more or less uncontrolled by reason; and will. The aim of the teacher is to instruct and guide all three. Uncontrolled feeling driving a weak will must wreck life. Therefore thought must be trained, instructed, and fitted to be the master of the person's destiny, the pilot of the soul. It will be the duty of the superintendent, as we shall see later, to give the Juniors the right material for thought, to fill eager minds with true conceptions, and to direct the awakening feelings and the growing will into right channels and toward noble purposes.

Instinct.—Instinct is an inherited tendency to perform certain acts when a definite stimulus is given. We find something corresponding to it in plants which seek the light, and of course in animals it is found everywhere. Samuel Butler calls it inherited memory; others have named it inherited capability or habit. Spencer says it resembles an organized memory. It shows itself in acts that are not reasoned, yet seem to serve a very clear purpose. The sucking babe is obeying an instinct. It has not learned and does not need to learn the art. A bee plunders flowers on its first flight. A chick is not many hours old before it makes darts at flies. Instincts are born with us, a fact which distinguishes them from habits, which are acquired.

But instincts are not always permanent; they sometimes fade away, and they can be overcome. No instinct is stronger than fear, yet we know that fear can be conquered. When an instinct is not given a chance to express itself, it will die out. All young chicks follow the mother hen, but incubator chicks very soon lose this tendency and are deaf to all clucking.

It is important that the Junior superintendent should know something about instincts and how to control them. They may be so indulged that they grow out of all reason: fear in this case becomes cowardice, pugnacity becomes bullying, and the perfectly correct instinct of self-protection may become selfishness. If properly directed fear will be under the control of the reason, pugnacity will become desire to defend the weak, and self-protection will be expanded to protection of others. This is a fair sample of what may be done with the instincts. Left alone and unguided they may run to seed; under control they lead to noble actions.

It should be remembered that the instincts are natural and serve a purpose, usually a good one. Fear is evidently intended to produce such instant action as will preserve the person from danger or hurt. If a weak animal did not show fear when it heard suspicious noises, it would not live long, for the strong would get it and sup upon its carcass. It is true that fear is of the jungle, but in the jungle it served a good end. When the need for it is past, however, it may become a handicap, a nervous source of constant trouble, and it easily degenerates into cowardice.

The aim of the superintendent is not to eliminate instincts, but to understand them and control them for the good of the child.

For example, one of the commonest instincts is the gregarious, the instinct to herd together. Children show this in marked degree. They do not like to be left alone. They greatly prefer to have an older person in the room with them. A little later this instinct manifests itself in the formation of clubs and societies. When it takes a wrong turn it leads to the gang. The cure is not the eradication of the instinct, but the organization of something better than the gang. But a superintendent would never think of this unless she knew something about the instinct which was at work in the child's life. That is why people sometimes stand aghast at a boy's inexplicable tendency to associate with the street-corner crowd. Good people should know a little about the boy's nature and feed his desires.

When a Junior society is proposed to a group of children of seven years old or more, the idea appeals to this instinct of gregariousness. They want to be with their kind in spite of the fact that they are individualists. Aristotle was not thinking about children, but he hit upon the reason for this instinct when he said that man needs society to provide him with opportunities to develop the most essential qualities of his own character and to furnish an outlet for his own proper activities. The lonely child cannot develop as he should, because nature has wisely ordained that full development shall take place in an environment in which there are other children. A large part of a child's education, in the home, in the school, and in the society, comes from the other children present. Children crave sympathy. They desire to show their powers. When they are happy their joy is increased when others are present to share it; when they are sad their pain is relieved if there are others to whom they can tell their woes.

Throughout the Junior age, that is, up to thirteen or thereabouts, children gravitate together and find pleasure in one another's company. Here are the roots of social life; friendships formed here will deepen in the teen years. The Junior society provides a fine opportunity to meet the child's need and give him his chance to grow along with others of his age.

It may be well to note that, as we have pointed out, while co-operation is difficult for children of Junior age, the beginnings of it are nevertheless present in them. The self is the child's centre, but his experience in the society makes him aware of the fact of others and he learns in his play that they must not merely be used but *played with*. Curiously enough co-operation grows out of competition; and the consciousness of the worth of others, the realization of *power added* in a game by annexing the strength and skill of a comrade, emerge out of the experience of competition. In the teen age the idea of competition persists, but the emphasis has changed. The boy finds himself a member of a team and he is with the team to win rather than out for himself.

We have already spoken of the play instinct and how play prepares the child for life. Curiosity is strong also. This is the basis of experimentation later in life, the root of scientific research. The superintendent will meet it and must respect and try to direct it, never to quench the flame or be impatient even when silly questions are asked.

The acquisitive instinct should be guided. Juniors should be encouraged to own things, for, through realization of their own position as owners, they learn to respect the ownership of others.

More important for the Junior superintendent is the instinct of construction manifested very strongly in the Junior age. Children want to make things. They want to master tools and handle materials. Very young children are content to make things without reference to the purpose to which they may be put, but in the Junior age the object in making things comes more and more to the front. Thus it is easy to get Juniors to paste picture postal cards back to back if they know that they are to be sent to children across the sea, but it would be hard if this work was called for without any explanation of the end in view. Construction work—that is, the making of scenes from Bible story in sand, clay, plasticene, pasteboard, and so on—makes a direct appeal to Juniors if the completed work has a chance to be used in the society's meetings. Work of this kind is in line with nature, and at the same time it fixes in the mind the lesson connected with the work.

Remember that children are moved by simple instincts and only by more complex emotions such as reverence, gratitude, and the like, as they grow older and gain experience. The superintendent's opportunity is to guide the elementary instincts and gradually establish those finer emotions that call for intelligence as well as instinct.

Habit.—Habits may be formed at all ages, but the years in which they are most easily formed are the Junior years from seven to twelve or thirteen. The physiological basis for habits is the nervous system. In every normal body there are two sets of nerves, the sensory nerves, which carry messages to the brain, and the motor nerves, which carry messages from the brain to all parts of the body and produce action. Besides this sensory-motor system there is another system called the sympathetic, which is more or less obscure, but which in some way seems to be connected with the condition of our vital organs and influences our emotions.

A thought or an act brings pleasure, let us say, to a child, and the thought or the act tends to repeat itself, for the child wants to experience the pleasure once more. Repetition forms habit, which is simply a tendency again to do certain things in the same way. The most familiar illustration of this is the wearing of a path through field or forest. The oftener one passes along it the better is the path worn. Thoughts and acts

THE CHILD

wear pathways in the mind, and thought and action travel easily over them.

Now one thing to note is that habits that bring pleasure are most easily formed. The mind vetoes the repetition of action which causes pain. To create a habit, therefore, make it pleasant, so that the Junior will want to do the thing again.

Interest is another factor in the creation of habits. What we do with force and enthusiasm makes a deeper impression than things we do listlessly. Therefore it is not enough to get children merely to repeat desirable acts which we wish to establish as habits, but to do them with earnestness and zeal.

When we speak of habit we think usually of actions, but habit is mental quite as much as physical, and for that part the mental habits are fully as important as the physical. To develop the habit of being loud-voiced is bad, but to develop that of being irritable is worse.

It is quite possible for Juniors to build up priceless attitudes toward their fellows. There is the habit of calmness, of the low voice, of patience, of gentleness, of optimism, of service, of unselfishness, of forgiveness, of seeing the good side of things. Then there is the habit of reading good books, Shakespeare, the Bible, biographies; the habit of prayer, of church attendance, of reverence, of worship, and of submission to the will of

God. If we cut paths like these in the minds of the Juniors they will rise in after years and call us blessed.

Every *incoming* impression passing to the brain awakens a response, or calls for an *outgoing* reply in the shape of some kind of expression. In adult life, and to some extent in the teen age, impulses which produce habits are usually chosen deliberately with an end in view; but the inexperience of the child makes impossible choice of this kind. Impulses rise within, of course, out of deep instincts, but most of the stimulus that creates habit comes from the environment. The child is not conscious of what is taking place. He receives suggestions from his surroundings, from what he sees others do, and he imitates what he sees. Very soon a habit is established. Here once more is the opportunity of the superintendent. Her personality, her manner, her tone, her general attitude, act as suggestions on the plastic mind of the Juniors, who imitate what they admire. And, of course, the superintendent can also stimulate the formation of good habits by her teaching and oral suggestion.

Discipline, by the way, in a Junior society is a habit. But this is a matter we must discuss elsewhere.

Finally, we must remember that habits are not isolated. They belong together as parts of one mentality, or one person. They jostle one another. As in a tropical forest trees struggle desperately to reach the light above, the strong attaining it by vigorous growth, the weak failing and fading away, so is it with habits. The strong survive. Those that are harmonious, that give pleasure, and that interest, survive. When a habit-seed is sown it must fight for its life, unless it is in harmony with other habits already established. To change the figure, when a new habit enters the mind it must either make its peace with habits already there, or overcome them. Character is a unit. Hence the more desirable habits we establish in the minds of Juniors the less chance there will be in later years for undesirable habits to gain a foothold. The good will overcome the evil. Discordant impressions will be rejected.

Wrong habits may be replaced by right ones. The child that holds a pen wrongly can be shown the proper way. The habit of speaking loudly can be overcome by the habit of speaking quietly. A habit tends to push out its opposite.

The method of establishing habits may be stated very briefly thus:

1. Enlist the desire and interest of the child. This brings about co-operation on the part of the Junior's will, which is the outgoing response to the suggestion that awakens his desire.

2. Seek to weaken undesirable habits by suppressing the acts connected with them. When habits are not repeated they die out.

3. Establish the desired habit by enthusiastic repetition.

These are the principles to apply. How to apply them will be a study in each instance.

QUESTIONS FOR REVIEW

What is the Junior age?
What should a Junior worker know about the child?
Why is a child's thought different from a grown-up person's?
Why should we not judge children by our own standards?
What are the characteristics of early childhood?
How does later childhood, 7 to 13, differ from early childhood?
Name some characteristics of later childhood.
How is the body developed in childhood?
What is meant by a child's "trying to experience the life he sees around him?"
What is suggestibility?
What are some mental characteristics of childhood?
What are the child's chief interests?
What is meant by thought, feeling, and will?
What is instinct? Illustrate it.
How can we guide the instincts and elevate them?
What instincts do children manifest?
What is habit? Illustrate it.
What is the difference between habit and instinct?
How can we create good habits?

CHAPTER III

MORALS AND RELIGION

Children are not born into this world with a full-fledged moral nature capable of immediately recognizing and choosing good and rejecting evil. What a child possesses as his inheritance is a capacity for making moral judgments. The seed of the moral life is present, but it needs time to grow and cultivation to bring it to maturity.

Education of the Moral Life.—For the child the education of the moral life begins when commands are laid upon it to do certain things, and it is prohibited from doing other things. The child must respond in some way to these commands and prohibitions; but his love for those giving the commands, usually his parents, and his instincts and habits, make obedience more or less easy. In this way the idea of duty is gradually built up. The parental commands are like scaffolding around a building; by and by it will be taken down and the work done with its aid will stand.

Such guidance as is given in commands and

rules will often seem irksome to a boy; but as intelligence expands, the meaning of the rules becomes plain and the boy begins to recognize moral principles which would apply even if there were no rules at all. The emphasis is shifted in late boyhood or early adolescence—the teen years— from external commands to inner conceptions about right and wrong. What was done in childhood because parent or teacher willed it, is now done *because it is right.* The value of careful training is seen in the intensity with which a youth clings to moral ideals that have been established in his earlier years.

What Morality Means to Children.—Our immediate interest, however, is in what morality means to a girl or boy of Junior age.

As we have already seen, children are often wilful, sometimes cruel, often thoughtless and wayward, and more or less uncontrolled in temper. They imitate the lives of adults, but without putting into their acts the thoughts and motives which adults put into theirs. Most of the faults of children are the faults of immature intelligence. "They know not what they do." Juniors may do much which older people call wrong, but the act will appear to the child in quite a different light; the evil motive will be lacking; and often the child will have difficulty in understanding why grown-ups make such a fuss about what seems to him such a harmless thing.

Take the Lying Habit.—It is notorious that many children often fail to tell the truth. Why? There may be various reasons. The child may be ignorant and be unable to say exactly what he has seen or heard. He may have imagined the things that he says, and be unable to distinguish between his imagination and the literal fact. He may have little or no realization of the nature of his fault. Or he may lie out of self-esteem or in self-defence. He wants to stand high in the opinion of others and the lie seems the easy road; or he may know and fear punishment and lie to escape it. There is usually a profound failure to understand the moral value of words. When an irate father or mother says, "You are lying and you know it," they speak the literal truth, but they forget that the child's *estimate* of his words is vastly different from theirs. And morality rests upon estimate; it is a system of values. The first step toward curing the evil of falsehood in a child is to understand the child's motive and patiently work toward building up a true estimate of falsehood and truth.

The same principle applies to other faults of childhood. If a child steals it is usually because its sense of property rights is not developed. If he destroys property, he is usually acting from some vague impulse, some suggestion or imagination, and without malice or understanding of the gravity of its offense. And herein lies one danger of the moving-picture theatre and yellow magazines, including the newspaper. The child finds in them suggestions which in favorable circumstances break into action. The sense of moral values is not yet powerful enough to check these wrong impulses.

The deep feelings that lie behind adult crime are not operative in children. The boy as a rule is not vindictive; he does not plan revenge. He soon forgets his anger and makes friends again easily.

Child Virtues.—Along with these faults there are in children a good many virtues. The child is ready to be led. He responds easily to love. He is a hero-worshipper and will imitate a good as readily as a bad example. He is teachable. He accepts the opinions of his elders or of those whom he respects. When he is told that he has done wrong he is willing to believe it; and often, when he repeats such an act, he is ready to make confession, provided he feels that he will not be misunderstood or drop in the esteem of the person to whom he confesses the wrong. There is grave danger that our adult attitude toward a child who confesses wrong-doing, or who is discovered in wrong-doing, may drive him to secretiveness, of which lying is merely a phase, or an attempt to cover up his wrong.

On the other hand, when children get the idea of right and wrong they soon appreciate the fact that wrong-doing should be punished. This is one of the lessons which superintendents should teach the Juniors. Sin and punishment are connected, *and the punishment is good for the sinner.* Juniors will see this and it may help them to "take their medicine."

One point to remember in the Junior age is that faults need not always be approached by the method of frontal attack. We can overcome them by crowding them out by their opposites. Irritableness can be conquered by establishing the habit of courtesy, and we shall make progress in the setting up of moral character if we can teach the Juniors to be honest, truthful (in spite of lapses), loyal, kind, sympathetic, and so forth.

Juniors, however, do not really comprehend abstract ideas. Our lessons must be put into concrete form. A lesson on truthfulness gets home to the heart if it is linked up with a story about one who is truthful.

The Child's Religion.—Without attempting an exhaustive analysis and definition of religion, we may say that fundamentally religion is the relation of the soul to God. The form that religion takes, and the effects it has on the life, depend upon how that relation is conceived. Men may have very wrong ideas about both God and their relation to Him, yet the fact that they conceive a relation at all is significant and calls for explanation.

Viewed from this angle religion is a state of mind. It is not something different from ordinary mental processes, thought, feeling, and will, but simply the application of these faculties to the conception of God and duty. If religion were a thing apart we should not need to study the mind of the child in order to teach it; but since it is the action of thought, feeling, and will in relation to the Eternal, it is clear that we must study these mental processes if we are to guide the child into true religious relations.

As we have already said, the religion of childhood is different from that of maturity, because the child is immature and his experiences are limited. Nevertheless, the religion of childhood is quite as real as that of manhood, although it is neither so deep nor so rich. Many of the conceptions of maturity are quite beyond the capacity of a child's mind. A boy or girl may understand simple sums in arithmetic, yet be at sea in higher mathematics. In religion it is the same. Inadequate conceptions will expand as intelligence grows.

The Junior readily absorbs the religious ideas presented to him. Answers to questions which appear woefully inadequate to the adult set the child's mind at rest. He will accept statements about God, heaven, eternity, sin, atonement, conversion, and so forth, with simple faith. He has not yet reached the questioning and doubting stage; that will come in adolescence or the teen years.

But just here lies a great danger. If a teacher takes the easy way and puts a child off with answers to his questions which he is bound to discover later are not true, nature will take revenge. For the youth in his teens will review those answers we give him in his Junior years. If he finds that some of them are false his faith in the others will be gravely shaken and he may reject all of them. The teaching that is given children should be simple enough for the child mind to grasp, and, while it must in the nature of the case be inadequate, it should be true as far as it goes. Moreover, the child should be taught that the answer given is not a full one and that a complete explanation is impossible until later in life. This will take the edge of much doubt and save him from many a shock.

The child's religion is *personal*. That is, his

attachment is to a person rather than to a doctrine. Hence children may be led definitely to accept Christ as their Saviour, Guide, Master, Friend, and they will try to follow Him. When they do this habits of great value are established that influence the whole after-life.

The kind of teaching given to children makes an impression that is carried forward into the teen years. When the teaching of childhood lays emphasis on sin and atonement, this teaching is likely to issue in adolescence in a definite type of conversion, if it issues in conversion at all. A different kind of teaching will produce a different kind of experience. This is why the religious instruction of childhood is transcendently important. Its influence persists.

QUESTIONS FOR REVIEW

How does the education of the child's moral life proceed?
What does morality mean to children?
What may a child's view of lying be?
What is the difference between many of childhood's sins and a grown-up's faults?
What are some of the child's virtues?
How may we teach and reinforce virtue?
What is religion?
How does the religion of childhood differ from that of maturity?
In teaching religion what ought we to guard against?

CHAPTER IV

THE SUPERINTENDENT'S TASK

The task of the superintendent is educational. Here is the child with latent capacities. In day school he receives instruction; in Sunday school he receives more instruction; what is to be the contribution of the Junior society to his equipment?

First of all, the greatest fact about the child is the fact of *personality*. It is this marvelous self that is to be trained. Whatever helps to develop the native powers of the self is good; whatever cramps, or hinders, or perverts these powers, is evil.

We have seen that children are impulsive in thought and act. True education will seek to bring about control in all directions. Education is more than the impartation of knowledge. It is more even than the conferring of mastery over intellect, emotion, and will. It is the development of character, the establishment of noble ideals. The superintendent's task is wider and deeper than that of a teacher. She is a character-maker, a builder of souls. Her starting-point will be the nature of the child, and the aim of her endeavor will be ethical, or the creation of right ideals and the power of self-control necessary to attain these ideals.

In a general way this is also the aim of the Sunday-school teacher, but the method is different. The Sunday school is predominantly a school of impression. Its main aim is to develop character by instruction. It fails of its mission if it does not impart knowledge of the Bible and the great facts of religion. But the society is predominantly a school of expression. It imparts knowledge, but not so much by teaching as by doing. It makes the child familiar with the Bible through memory work and drills—that is, through handling the book. Its appeal to the intellect is not by way of imparting knowledge, but by training the child to think for himself. The emphasis is upon *action*.

There are thus a few general principles which may help the superintendent in training Juniors. Most of them have already been treated, but we may summarize them thus:

1. The Junior should be approached through his interest. The superintendent should try to keep within the experience of the child when making any appeal. Whatever arouses interest, —story, drawing, or object,—forms a point of contact without which words are idle.

THE SUPERINTENDENT'S TASK 51

2. In teaching children we should begin with the concrete rather than the abstract. You will probably fail if you try to interest a child in botany; but if you show him a flower and explain its beauties, you get his interest at once and he will follow you wherever you will. In morals and religion it is the same. Use concrete examples, stories, incidents. As the Junior's intelligence grows he will gain facility in grasping abstract truth.

3. The superintendent will make use of the fact that Juniors are ready to receive truth on the authority of the instructor. At the same time she will use as little dogmatic authority as possible. Thus, when a Junior offers a manifestly wrong explanation of anything, the superintendent should not crush him by sheer weight of authority, but try to enlighten the mind and show how the opinion does not fit the facts. Even then care is needed lest we harm the sensitive soul. Rather try to find something of truth in the explanation, praise that, and make this the point of departure for a fuller, truer statement. We need tact.

4. The superintendent should encourage the Juniors to think for themselves. Education fails if it does not turn out men and women who have command of their intellectual powers and can think things through for themselves. It is easy to

be lazy in one's thinking, and therefore hazy in one's thought. We begin enterprises without thinking them to the end, without counting the cost. We shall do Juniors a great service if we can lead them to think clearly, to make reasoned decisions, and to carry out their purposes. Their attempts may at first be faltering and even futile, but they will be gaining power. A question given to a Junior to answer in the meeting, if it is given a week in advance, is a fine method of teaching by expression.

5. Children live in a concrete and interesting world. Has it no message for them? We believe it has, and that they can be led to enjoy nature and find in it traces of the Creator's wisdom. Connect nature with God. He made it, controls it, and it speaks of Him; His footsteps are seen everywhere. Such teaching is developed more fully in the teen age and is very valuable.

6. The child is a bundle of instincts, as we have seen, all of them good until perverted. The superintendent will need a working knowledge of these instincts and learn how to guide them aright. The center of the instincts is the self. Self-preservation is good; but when it is perverted and becomes selfishness it is bad. The Juniors must be taught what is due to themselves and also what is pure selfishness. Personality is sacred and must be guarded like a precious possession.

THE SUPERINTENDENT'S TASK 53

Study the section on instincts and think of how to make use of them—curiosity, memory, desire to make things. Handwork in the society (explained in a booklet published by the United Society of Christian Endeavor, "Handwork for Juniors"), makes a strong appeal and has educational value.

7. Establish right habits in the child. There are the habits of daily prayer, of reading the Bible daily, of memorizing a Bible verse every day, of courtesy, of doing a good turn every day, of obedience, and so forth.

8. Then there are work and play. Recreation should be part of the programme of the society. Socials, picnics, hikes, games, athletics should be carried out under the leadership of the superintendent and her assistants. Emphasis should be placed on the value of doing chores in the home that the habit of seeing and performing everyday duties may be achieved.

9. Think of the effect of the superintendent's personality. It is hardly too much to say that what a superintendent teaches is less important than what she *is*. Both children and youths form strong attachments to their teachers and imitate them. Juniors will reflect the traits of the superintendent. Example is powerful.

10. Can we make the Juniors realize the presence of Christ in the Junior meeting? We believe

this is possible. They will have no difficulty with the fact that He is invisible. For them, if they are taught so, He will be present, and they will look upon Him with devotion and love. He should always be held up as the Great Example. Children will love the superintendent, but they will adore Christ; they will admire her, but Him they will worship.

11. Discipline must be maintained in a Junior meeting. The great obstacle is the restlessness of the children. It is hard for them to sit still. There are so few checks between their thoughts and their actions that they are in perpetual motion. It is obvious that nothing can be accomplished in a buzz of conversation or the fidgeting of a crowd.

First of all, gain the attention of the Juniors. There are two ways of doing this. The first method is external, the ringing of a bell, or the slamming of a ruler on the desk. The sudden noise startles the Juniors and for a brief moment drives out other thoughts. But the noise begins again, and by and by even the exasperated slamming of the ruler on the desk makes no impression at all.

The second method makes its appeal to the mind. It touches the springs of interest. Perhaps it is some quiet statement that connects itself with a common interest. Perhaps it is nothing but the appearing of the superintendent in her place.

For Discipline Is a Habit.—If the Juniors are taught to be still the moment the superintendent takes her place, just as the church is hushed when the pastor enters the pulpit, they will be still. It may take both time and effort to establish this habit. The reason for it should be explained over and over again until it becomes a part of the child's very being. The reason is that the meeting is a part of the divine service; that God is truly present; and that in His presence we must be reverent. Whatever will conduce to give the children a sense of the Presence will help discipline. The opening service should have this as its one aim—always: silent prayer; the repetition of some Scripture verse like, "The Lord is in his holy temple, let all the earth keep silence before him."

Again, a basis for discipline is love for the superintendent. Children do not willingly hurt or vex those they love.

Then, of course, there are other aids which are perfectly legitimate. The assistant superintendents are a great help. One superintendent may manage a small society, but if the society is large or the majority of the children are under nine, it is difficult for the superintendent to control it all the time. Several assistants should be present to help. Members of the Senior society may be enlisted to serve.

Also, put some responsibility for discipline on the Juniors themselves. Make some of the older ones monitors. Seat the children in rows with a monitor at the end of each row. The monitors should have deportment books in which to keep a record of the behavior of the Juniors in their charge. In contests deportment should be made a principal point and marks should be given for it.

A grave question is what to do with the boy or girl who does not respond to discipline. In the first place we must rid our minds of the adult conception of badness. A restless boy is not necessarily bad. He is not necessarily bad when he is mischievous. In lack of discipline there is rarely any malice. Often it has been possible to enlist such a boy on the side of order by the simple expedient of giving him something to do, even making him a monitor and holding him responsible for the behavior of others.

If this fails take him aside—but take care that the other Juniors do not see it—and have a heart to heart talk with him. Invite him to your home, feed him, and then have a chat with him. Take him gently. Explain kindly the necessity of order. Appeal to his chivalry.

THE SUPERINTENDENT'S TASK 57

If the first talk does not help, try another. If that brings no improvement there are two other steps to take.

First, you may go to the child's parents and tell the facts. This should not be done, however, unless you are positive that you can do so with tact and sympathy. Parents naturally think that their children can do no wrong, or not much wrong, and their instinct is to defend the child. On the other hand a mother very soon sees whether or not a superintendent loves her child. If she is convinced that the superintendent loves the child, she will listen and co-operate gladly. A visit to parents therefore should only follow the most earnest and honest heart-searching. Unless you can win the parents it is best not to go near them to complain about boy or girl. In any case do not complain. Praise the child's good points. Tell of the use he might be in the society if he could only be a little more orderly. Show that you want him and need him.

If, after all this, the evil continues and your work is being nullified the next thing to do is to carry the problem to the pastor. Tact is needed here also. The whole situation should be explained and help asked. Possibly the presence of the pastor in a few meetings might cure the trouble. If not, follow his advice in dealing with the boy. If the child must be expelled that the society may not be made useless, this step should be taken only by the pastor. He should come and explain the matter to the Juniors. He should also explain it to the parents. A matter so serious as this should have the highest sanction, and the Juniors should feel its seriousness.

Fortunately this extreme step will not often be necessary. The superintendent will endure a good deal before she will resort to it.

Some superintendents have solved the problem by getting a young man from the Senior society to take half a dozen of the most restless boys and after the opening exercises, teach them in another room.

One superintendent tried this method. She holds a weekly social hour with games, singing, and so on, every Saturday afternoon. There are a number of assistants in this society and they take turns in helping. This social hour is for members of the society only—special socials being held for outsiders. When a boy or girl misbehaves the punishment is that he is told he must not come to the following weekly social hour. This has had an excellent effect. The Juniors have the best of times on these social occasions and forego them only reluctantly.

Even when a weekly social is not possible, the

THE SUPERINTENDENT'S TASK 59

principle may be applied. When the Juniors understand that misbehavior means that they will be barred from the next social, they will think twice before they "cut up." The superintendent must be firm and carry through this stern discipline, if she hopes to succeed.

What to Teach. Sometimes a Junior superintendent asks the question, What shall I teach the Juniors? What kind of subjects do they most need? Here is a list, not complete by any means, but suggestive. Emphasis should be put on the positive virtues, but the opposite vices are given in case the superintendent should desire to use them by way of warning.

Virtues

FOR THE BODY

1. Tidiness, cleanliness.
2. Exercise, play, **work**, skill.

FOR THE MIND

1. Self-control.
2. Prudence.
3. Courage.
4. Industry.
5. Accuracy and thoroughness.
6. Perseverance.

Vices

FOR THE BODY

1. Untidiness, dirt.
2. Laziness, inaptitude.

FOR THE MIND

1. Impulsiveness.
2. Imprudence.
3. Cowardice.
4. Indolence, laziness.
5. Inaccuracy, carelessness, superficiality.
6. Instability.

Virtues
FOR THE MIND

Vices
FOR THE MIND

(Continued)

7. Patience.
8. Self-reliance.
9. Reason.
10. Fidelity.
11. Making collections.
12. Purposefulness, apprehension of ends.
13. Will and choice.
14. Imitation.
15. Curiosity and how to gratify it.
16. Use of the memory.
17. Using the imagination.
18. Calmness.
19. Gentleness.
20. Hopefulness, optimism.
21. Unselfishness.
22. Service.
23. Courtesy.
24. Reading good books.
25. Confession of wrongdoing.
26. Sympathy and pity.
27. Humility.
28. Meekness.
29. Ambition to learn.
30. Clean speech.

7. Impatience.
8. Too much dependence on others.
9. No thought for consequences.
10. Unfaithfulness.
11. No hobbies.
12. Drifting.
13. Influenced by others.
14. Imitation of evil.
15. Stupidity.
16. An empty mind.
17. Lack of wit.
18. Excitability, anger.
19. Roughness.
20. Despair, pessimism.
21. Selfishness.
22. Doing nothing for others.
23. Boorishness.
24. Reading bad books.
25. Secretiveness.
26. Cruelty or indifference.
27. Pride.
28. Boasting.
29. Indolence.
30. Foul speech.

THE SUPERINTENDENT'S TASK

Virtues	Vices
FOR SOCIAL LIFE	FOR SOCIAL LIFE

1. Obedience.	1. Disobedience.
2. Respect and reverence.	2. Disrespect, irreverence.
3. Truthfulness.	3. Lying.
4. Honesty.	4. Dishonesty.
5. Courtesy and manners.	5. Boorishness.
6. Helpfulness at home (chores, etc.).	6. Shirking duties.
7. Love.	7. Hate.
8. Justice.	8. Injustice.
9. Kindness.	9. Cruelty.
10. Generosity.	10. Giving nothing away.
11. Co-operation.	11. Individualism.
12. Friendliness.	12. Quarrelsomeness.
13. Loyalty.	13. Disloyalty.
14. Patriotism.	14. Without love of country.
15. Possession, acquisition.	15. Stealing.
16. Gregariousness (love of company).	16. Careless of others.
17. Constructiveness.	17. Destructiveness.

FOR THE SOUL	FOR THE SOUL
1. Worship and reverence.	1. Irreverence.
2. Obedience.	2. Disobedience.
3. Faith.	3. Disbelief.
4. Love.	4. Hate.
5. Prayer.	5. No recognition of God.
6. Praise.	6. Temper.
7. Church-going.	7. Non-church-going.

Virtues	Vices
FOR THE SOUL	FOR THE SOUL
(Continued)	
8. Love of the beautiful in nature.	8. Blindness to beauty in nature.
9. Love of beauty in art.	9. Blindness in art.
10. Love of beauty in conduct.	10. Blindness in conduct.
11. Love of beauty in character.	11. Blindness in character.

Then, of course, there are Bible subjects, such as God, the life beyond, sin, conversion, repentance, fear, lust, irritableness, gossip, vindictiveness, revenge, and so on.

QUESTIONS FOR REVIEW

What is the task of the superintendent?
How does the superintendent's task differ from that of a Sunday-school teacher?
What are some principles to remember in dealing with Juniors?
What is the external method of discipline?
What is the internal method?
What are some fundamentals of discipline?
What should be done with the child who does not respond to discipline?
How may we use the social life of the society to buttress discipline?
Name some topics that should be taught to Juniors.

CHAPTER V

QUALIFICATIONS OF THE SUPERINTENDENT

Most young women or young men who are willing to learn may become efficient superintendents. Since the church has no school for training superintendents, those that have had a general training in the Senior society as a rule will have a sound foundation of knowledge of method upon which to build. For the rest, experience will come.

We do not look for perfection in Junior superintendents any more than we do in Sunday-school teachers. But there are certain qualifications that may be looked for.

The first is love.—No one can be a real success with children who does not love them. On the other hand love of children grows on one the closer we get to them. And, by the way, there is a fine reward in this; for the more we love childhood, the greater becomes our capacity to love not only human beings but God himself. One of the commonest sorts of soul-poverty is a lack of capacity to love. Without that capacity we cannot love God. But dealing with children expands our ability to love, and so rewards us by opening channels through which the love of God may flow into our hearts.

The second requirement is personality.—Personality is the full self, the sum of our thoughts and ambitions. A warm and loving personality radiates a benignant influence. It is also a magnet, and attracts. Personality is a living and growing reality, expanding with the years that pass. The superintendent that impresses her ideals on the Juniors and leads them to look up to her with love is moulding their lives in a wonderful way through her personality.

The superintendent should be patient.—Children can be exasperating at times, but the superintendent must not get irritated or grow discouraged. She must be gentle under provocation, amiable, no matter how troublesome the Juniors may be, kind to the unworthy, and persevering in her patience. The Junior society may be quite as much an education for the superintendent as for the Juniors. This is another of the unrecognized rewards of the superintendent. The society builds up her own character as she builds up the character of the children.

The superintendent who flies into a rage will fail. How can she teach self-control when she does not practise it? To maintain discipline she must be calm, serene, master of the situation. She should never enter a Junior meeting without preparation of heart that she may be braced to meet whatever situation may arise.

She must be just.—It is fatal to discriminate or play favorites. All must be alike to her, the bad (if we may use this term about children) as well as the good. Indeed the ones that are difficult to manage should receive special attention. Often the badness of a child is nothing but a fine instinct or energy gone wrong.

Consecration is another prerequisite for a successful superintendent.—She is a shepherd of souls. She is to these children what the pastor is to the church. She is more, for she comes into closer contact with them than the pastor does with his congregation. She knows them better, for she talks more with them, and they are less secretive than the average grown-up. Her influence is constantly upon them. She is in a sense master of their destinies. If she does her work well, the children of these children will feel it, without knowing it. If she does her work poorly, an unborn generation will suffer loss.

I magnify the office of superintendent. It calls for whole-hearted consecration and clear vision.

It calls for tact, of course.—She will need tact to attract to her a group of enthusiastic assistants. The demand that a Senior society elect a Junior committee usually fails; but a warm-hearted superintendent can make others see her vision and come to her aid. She will need tact in working with them too, tact in consultation and co-operation.

Finally, there is knowledge.—A superintendent may begin with little knowledge of how to carry on a Junior society, but she must try to accumulate more. She should as far as possible apply the principles of the Senior society to Junior work, modified, of course, to meet the needs of children. We shall speak of helps later.

The society's work will drive the superintendent to her Bible. This is clear gain to her and is another of those unrecognized rewards. A superintendent gets out of a Junior society more than she puts in.

Pastor superintendents.—Not many pastors are superintendents, and as a rule should not be; for it is better for a pastor to oversee the work done by others than be loaded down with too

QUALIFICATIONS 67

many duties. A pastor's wife makes an excellent superintendent and many are filling this position. It is essential, when this is so, that she should surround herself with assistants, so that there may be some young people trained to take her place when her husband moves to another church.

QUESTIONS FOR REVIEW

Name the qualifications of a Junior superintendent?
Why is love the first qualification?
What is meant by personality?
What is the effect of impatience on a Junior society?
What dangers lurk in a superintendent's favoritism?
What is consecration?
What is tact?
How should the superintendent study her Bible?
Should pastors or pastors' wives be Junior superintendents?

CHAPTER VI

ORGANIZATION AND EQUIPMENT

Before attempting to organize a Junior society the superintendent should familiarize herself with the method of conducting a meeting and carrying on committee work.

If no one is willing to be superintendent, the Senior society may appoint a Junior committee of three or four members and place responsibility for the work on them. Sometimes such a group divides up the work so that two of the group are present every Sunday, the other two being free. In this case, however, one of the two who are on duty should have been present the week before, so that there may be a measure of continuity in the programme. The best arrangement, however, is to have as superintendent one who will be present at every meeting, the others being assistants.

The steps to be taken to organize a Junior society are these:

1. Get the pastor's permission to start a society and seek his aid.

2. Secure assistants from the Senior society if

ORGANIZATION AND EQUIPMENT 69

possible. Some Junior societies which have been conducted by persons who have never belonged to a Christian Endeavor society fail to carry out the Christian Endeavor principle and become mission bands or something of that sort.

3. Secure the Juniors. Two methods may be pursued. First, an attempt may be made to launch the society with the greatest possible publicity and get as many charter members as possible under the impulse of this initial enthusiasm. In that case the call for Juniors to attend an organizing meeting should be given through the church bulletin, from the pulpit, in the Sunday school, and adult members of the church and church organizations should be asked to send children to the meeting. Letters may be written to parents, newspaper advertising may be used, and an announcement may be posted on the church bulletin-board. Perhaps a social for children should be tried.

When the children come, the superintendent should carefully explain what the society is and how it is conducted. She should read the active member's pledge and explain it clause by clause. A constitution should be ready and should also be read and explained. At the close a copy of the pledge should be given to each Junior present. This they will take home and bring it signed to the next meeting. The following Sunday morning the pastor will explain to the congregation what has been done and how they may help the Juniors to sign and keep the pledge. A favorable atmosphere is a great asset to a new society.

Some workers prefer to have all begin as preparatory members, in which case the preparatory member's pledge should be used. This is the better method unless one knows the Juniors well.

At the second meeting the signed pledge cards are collected and those Juniors who turn them in are considered charter members. The superintendent will then propose the names of carefully selected Juniors as president, vice-president, secretary, and treasurer. She may appoint chairmen of committees at this meeting if she will. This meeting will close with a short devotional service. The following week the names of members on all the committees will be posted on the wall and special committee meetings will be arranged for under the guidance of the superintendent and her assistants.

The second method is to select from six to a dozen Juniors who seem to be leaders of the young folks and invite them to your home. When they come explain to them your idea of forming a Junior society; show and explain to them both pledge and constitution. They will sign the pledge either now or at a second meeting. Out of this group elect officers and chairmen of committees. This will bring into being a skeleton society.

Then adopt publicity measures to attract other

Juniors. If there is any sentiment about the privilege of being charter members, keep the charter membership open for a week or two to give others a chance to come in.

The Assistants.—As a rule try to have several assistants. If you wish to win the boys get a young man from the Senior society to be one of your helpers. His special duty will be not only to help to keep discipline, but to work with the boys during the week. When handwork is done, he will be leader to show the boys how to do it; he will organize athletics, games, baseball club, and at socials, picnics, and on hikes he will be indispensable. He may be made superintendent of play and recreation activities. Boys like to attend track meets and are won through their play instinct.

To each assistant should be assigned definite duties. The work done by Junior committees depends on the leadership of older people. The assistants should have charge of the committee work, several committees being assigned to each assistant. These helpers will plan with the committee chairmen the work of the committee month by month; they will attend the committee meetings, but must not conduct them; let the Juniors do that themselves. The superintendent and assistants will meet, of course, and lay out the work for the whole season. In this way the society's work may be unified and every part of the society will be working with the other parts.

The assistants may be used in the regular meetings too. One may have charge of all the society's memory work; another may have charge of all mission study; another will guide the handwork; another may help the Junior secretary and assist in getting up Junior posters for advertising the meeting. A society organized in this way cannot fail of success.

The Membership.—When a society is started the superintendent should try to bring in children between the ages of seven and twelve. Those above this age will gravitate to the Intermediate society; but if there is no Intermediate society Juniors up to thirteen or thereabouts may come into the Junior group. Sometimes there are younger children who want to be counted in too. They may be accepted as preparatory members. If it is found that they are too young to follow the topic, or if they are restless and hard to manage, give them a name, "Sunbeams," or such like, and let an assistant superintendent take them to another room after the opening exercises and teach them the topic.

The Active Member's Pledge.—This reads:

ORGANIZATION AND EQUIPMENT

> Trusting in the Lord Jesus Christ for strength, I promise Him that I will strive to do whatever He would like to have me do, that I will pray and read the Bible every day, and that, just so far as I know how, I will try to lead a Christian life. I will be present at every meeting of the society when I can, and will take some part in every meeting.
>
> Name........................
>
> I am willing that...............should sign this pledge, and will do all I can to help.......... keep it.
>
> Parent's name......................
>
> Residence ....

The Preparatory Member's Pledge:

Preparatory Members are those who wish to belong to the society, but whose parents are not quite ready to let them sign the pledge. They will be expected to attend the meetings regularly, and it is hoped that this will be considered simply as a preparation for active membership.

The preparatory members shall take the following pledge:

> As a preparatory member I promise to be present at every meeting when I can, and to be quiet and reverent during the meeting.
>
> Signed........................

74   JUNIOR WORKERS' MANUAL

The Constitution.—This follows closely the constitutions of the Intermediate and Senior societies. This is advisable so that the training of the boys and girls may follow similar lines in all grades of Christian Endeavor.

Article I.—Name.

This society shall be called the JUNIOR SOCIETY OF CHRISTIAN ENDEAVOR OF ....
....

Article II.—Object.

Its object shall be to promote an earnest Christian life among the boys and girls who shall become members, and prepare them for the active service of Christ.

Article III.—Membership.

1. The members shall consist of two classes, Active and Preparatory.*

2. *Active Members.* Any boy or girl between the ages of......and......, inclusive, who shall be approved by the Superintendent and Assistant, may become an Active member of the society by taking the following pledge:

(Pledge quoted on preceding page.)

---
*NOTE—Some societies also provide for Honorary members, consisting of the Pastor, President of the Senior Society, and mothers that are especially interested in the society and desire to help it by their prayers and occasional attendance.

Article IV.—Officers.

The officers of the society shall be one or more Superintendents chosen by the Senior Society, with the approval of the church and Pastor; also a President, Vice-President, Secretary and Treasurer, who shall be chosen by the boys and girls. There shall also be a Lookout Committee, a Prayer-Meeting Committee, a Social Committee, a Missionary Committee, and such other committees as the Superintendents may deem best. These committees shall be nominated by the Superintendents and elected by the society.

Article V.—Duties of Officers.

1. The *Superintendent* shall have full control of the society.
2. The *Assistant Superintendent* shall aid the Superintendent in her work.
3. The *President* shall conduct the business meetings, under the direction of the Superintendent.
4. The *Vice-President* shall act in the absence of the President.
5. The *Secretary* shall keep a correct list of the members, take the minutes of the business meetings and call the names at the roll-call meetings.

6. The *Treasurer* shall take up the collections, enter the amount in the account-book, and turn over the money to the Assistant Superintendent, and also enter all expenditures as directed by the Superintendent.

Article VI.—Duties of Committees.

1. The *Lookout Committee* shall secure the names of any who may wish to join the society, and report the same to the Superintendents for action. They shall also obtain excuses from members absent from the roll-call, and affectionately look after and reclaim any who seem indifferent to their pledge.

2. The *Prayer-Meeting Committee* shall, in connection with the Superintendent, select topics, assign leaders, and do what it can to secure faithfulness to the prayer-meeting pledge.

3. The *Social Committee* shall welcome the children to the meetings, and introduce them to the other members of the society. They may also arrange for occasional sociables.

Article VII.—Relationship.

The Junior society is a part of the church, and its relation to the Senior Young People's Society should be close and intimate. It is expected that when the members of the Junior society have reached their age limit, they will enter the Senior Society as Active members.

Article VIII.—Meetings.

1. A prayer meeting shall be held once every week. A consecration meeting shall be held once a month, at which the pledge shall be read and the roll called, and the responses of the members shall be considered a renewal of the pledge of the society. If any member is absent from three consecutive consecration meetings, without excuse, his name may be dropped from the list of members.

2. Part of the hour of the weekly meeting may, if deemed best, be used by the Pastor or Superintendent of the society for instruction in the Bible, doctrines, manners, or morals, or for other exercises which they may approve.

BY-LAWS*

1. The society shall hold a prayer meeting on ....of each week. The last regular meeting of each month shall be a consecration meeting. The business meeting may be held in con-

---

*It is hoped that so far as possible the societies will adhere to the Model Constitution, making all necessary local changes in the By-laws.

nection with the first regular meeting of each month.

2. The officers and committees shall be chosen in ....and............and continue six months, beginning on the first of the month following their election.

3. Special meetings of the society may be held at any time, at the call of the Superintendent.

4. A collection shall be taken at the consecration meeting, and at the other meetings if desired, the money thus obtained to be held available for benevolent objects and to meet the expenses of the society.

5. All committees should meet at least once a month for consultation with the Superintendent in regard to their work.

6. All expenditures shall be made under the direction of the Superintendent.

7. Other committees may be added, whose duties shall be defined as follows:

The *Music Committee* shall distribute and collect the singing-books, and co-operate with the leader of the meeting in trying in every way to make the singing a success.

The *Missionary Committee* shall arrange for an occasional missionary meeting, and seek to interest the members in home and foreign work.

The *Temperance Committee* shall arrange for an occasional temperance meeting, and circulate a tem-

ORGANIZATION AND EQUIPMENT 79

perance pledge among the members.

The *Sunday-School Committee* shall secure the names of children who do not attend Sunday school, and invite them to become members of the Sunday school.

The *Flower Committee* shall provide flowers for the Sunday-School room, and distribute fruit and flowers to the sick and needy.

The *Scrap-Book Committee* shall collect pictures and clippings, and make scrap-books for sick and disabled members and for distribution in the hospitals.

The *Relief Committee* shall collect clothing for the destitute children found in the Sunday school and society, and bring it to the Superintendent for distribution.

The *Birthday Committee* shall report all birthdays as they occur among the members, so that special prayer may be offered for each member on his or her birthday.

8. This Constitution and By-laws may be altered or amended any time the Superintendents and Pastor find it necessary.

The Equipment.—Superintendent and assistants will get books and pamphlets on Christian Endeavor work, together with *The Junior Christian Endeavor World* and *The Christian Endeavor World*. Each committee should make a scrap-book and in it paste all plans for work which that committee can secure from these and other papers or books.

The superintendents of Junior societies in a city or town should frequently meet to discuss problems of their work. Junior workers should attend Junior Endeavor conventions and meet Junior workers from other districts.

Society Equipment.—Song books will be needed. The Juniors will want the Junior song book, "Junior Carols," published by the United Society of Christian Endeavor, Boston, Mass.

The more you get Juniors to read Christian Endeavor papers the more interest will they manifest. Form a club of Junior subscribers to *The Junior Christian Endeavor World*. It is indispensable.

The United Society also publishes Junior Expert leaflets, one leaflet for each officer and for each committee. These leaflets outline work for officers and committees. Every Junior should have the leaflet explaining the work of the committee of which he is a member. These leaflets are bound in book form, "The Junior Text-Book." When a Junior studies this book and passes an examination in it he is granted a degree, "Junior Christian Endeavor Expert."

The society will need topic cards. Every member should also be given a copy of "Junior Prayer-

ORGANIZATION AND EQUIPMENT 81

Meeting Topics and Daily Portion." This is a booklet costing only a few cents, which contains the topics and a Scripture reading for every day.

Some equipment for memory work will be necessary and may be obtained from the United Society. Juniors enjoy memory work. It comes easy to them. The mind craves exercise as well as the body, and it gets it in this way. Bible texts stored in the heart in youth are never utterly forgotten.

The society should have a Junior Training Chart (supplied by the United Society). It contains a fine outline of work for a society, a programme which superintendents may follow with profit. It covers work in the meeting and work for committees.

A Christian Endeavor wall-pledge is also needed so that the Juniors may have the pledge constantly before them and repeat it every time new members are taken into the society, and at consecration meetings.

It will pay a society to purchase a blackboard if the church has not one for the children. As a substitute large sheets of paper hung on the wall may be used.

If the cost of these things seems formidable, there is no reason why the Senior society should not help to buy them. To equip a Junior society is surely a missionary undertaking. If the Juniors can do it, however, it is well to allow them to pay the bills. They find pleasure in working for definite objects and they may take better care of equipment for which they have worked and paid.

QUESTIONS FOR REVIEW

What should a superintendent know about Junior work before organizing a society?
In organizing, what steps should first be taken?
Describe two methods of securing the Juniors for a society?
What publicity is advisable?
Why are several assistant superintendents or helpers needed?
How may different duties be assigned to assistants?
Who should be members of a Junior society?
What is the difference between the Junior and Senior pledge?
Who are preparatory members? Why have them?
What is the value of a constitution?
How should a constituion be adopted?
What equipment does a society need for its work?
Where may equipment be secured?
Who may help in paying for equipment?

CHAPTER VII

THE OFFICERS

Care should be taken in the selection of officers. Choose only those who will try to do the work; as a rule they will be older Juniors.

The President.—The president may be either a boy or a girl. The duties are to preside at the business meetings and to plan, along with the superintendent, the work of the society. He has oversight of the whole society and if any committee is not doing its work, he should talk to the chairman and try to help him. The superintendent will teach him how to encourage the workers. At the business meetings he will need help to make out a schedule of business and to carry on the meeting in proper form, as suggested in the President's Efficiency Leaflet. He is supposed to keep the work moving and should suggest simple things for the society to do.

The Vice-President.—In small societies a vice-president may not be needed, unless as an understudy for president. He should consider himself the president's helper. He will occasionally preside at business meetings. It is a good plan to make him chairman of the lookout committee. He will be ready in the meetings to do whatever the president or superintendent asks him to do.

The Secretary.—The secretary will keep the society's roll in order. She will call the roll at consecration meetings, will write all letters which the society sends officially, will receive letters for the society, and will consult the superintendent as to what to do with them. She will keep the minutes of business meetings and of executive committee meetings; she will receive from the chairmen of committees their written reports and will keep them in a file; and she will keep an index in her minute-book to help her to find any action taken in past meetings.

Many societies keep a card index instead of a membership roll. The secretary will keep this up to date. Each card should contain the name and address of a Junior, his age, and the date of joining the society; perhaps also his father's name. The card will state what position the Junior occupies in the society, what offices he has held, and the dates of them, what committees he has served on, whether or not he is a member of the church, and his record of attendance.

THE OFFICERS

These cards will tell the whole story of the Junior's relation to the society.

The Treasurer.—The treasurer's duty is not merely to receive money from the members, but to devise ways and means of getting the money. The superintendent will get him an account book and show him how to enter on one side all money received, and on the other side all money expended. He will be instructed to pay out no money unless authorized to do so by the superintendent and the president. Some superintendents take upon themselves the duties of secretary and treasurer, thinking that the most efficient way of conducting the society's business is the best. We must remember that the society is a training school and that Juniors are learning to do things *by doing them.* We must give them the opportunity.

The superintendent will help the treasurer to make a budget for the society. He will write down on a piece of paper all the money that the society may be expected to spend during the year. Thus:

Current expenses ....$
Home missions ....$
Foreign missions ....$
For socials ....$
For the church........................$

For song books ....$
For the sick ....$
For flowers ....$

Add to these items other causes as desired.

Then on another sheet of paper write down the expected income of the society.

From pledges ....$
From collections ....$
From socials ....$
Missionary gifts ....$

The money received in the past year will suggest sources of income. At the annual meeting of the society this budget should be written on the blackboard and explained to the Juniors, who should be encouraged to pledge what they can toward the total amount.

The treasurer will place a number before each Junior's name in his book. He will give to the Juniors envelopes with numbers corresponding to those opposite their names, and in these envelopes the Juniors will make their weekly or monthly gifts, which the treasurer will credit to them.

Every three months the treasurer may give to each Junior a statement of what he has paid and what he still owes on his pledge. When a Junior falls behind in his payments the treasurer should remind him that he has neglected to pay and report the reason to the superintendent.

THE OFFICERS 87

Some Junior societies have regular dues, so much a month. Others rely on loose collections each Sunday. The pledging plan seems superior to these because it has elements of training in, it which neither of the other plans have. The habit of making a pledge and paying it is a good one to form.

With the superintendent's consent other plans for getting money may be tried. A glass jar may be placed on the table at each meeting and the Juniors may fill it with pennies. A birthday box may be kept and Juniors that have had birthdays during the previous week may put into it as many pennies as they are years old. Mite boxes may be given to the Juniors to fill at home. Juniors are sometimes given ten cents and told to trade with the money and bring the profit to the society. Juniors may be encouraged to earn some of the money they give to the society. Money is earned by doing chores, cutting grass on lawns, running errands, selling popcorn, conducting a booth at a social or a bazaar, selling Christmas cards, selling photographs, and so forth.

The treasurer should be taught to keep the society's money apart from his own and never use it for private purposes on any pretext whatever. He will pay bills and get receipts, but if money is to be sent by mail he may give the amount to the superintendent who will send it.

Executive-Committee Meeting.—The executive committee consists of the officers of the society and the chairmen of all committees. They should meet once a month or once every two months to discuss plans for the society's work. The superintendent or assistants will always be present to render aid, but the Juniors themselves should be allowed to conduct the meeting in proper parliamentary form. The superintendent may give suggestions to officers and chairmen of committees before the meeting so that they may have worth-while proposals to make.

To this meeting the chairman of each committee will bring a written report which will tell briefly what the committee he represents set out to do a month or two months previously, what has been accomplished, and if the work has not been completed, the report will tell the reason why. The report should also outline the work the committee intends to do in the coming month or two. These reports the secretary will file.

The president will make out an order of business something like this: 1. Opening song and prayer. 2. Reading of the minutes of the last meeting. 3. Reports of officers and committee chairmen. 4. Business arising out of these reports. 5. New business. This will include plans for work.

The Society's Business Meeting.—A business meeting of the society may be held every two or three months—oftener if found necessary. A programme for the meeting should be made out by the president, with the aid of the superintendent. The business meeting should always be preceded by an executive-committee meeting where the order of business may be discussed. This order will be much the same as in an executive committee meeting, except that the chairmen of committees will not give reports. The secretary's report will tell what the committees have done. The treasurer, however, should make a separate report. Then will come a brief statement of plans for work which the Juniors will be asked to adopt by vote.

Do not crowd this meeting with small details. These should be settled in the executive-committee meeting. The president will, of course, preside.

Never hold a business meeting after a Sunday prayer meeting. Hold it rather on a week evening or afternoon, and serve refreshments. More Juniors will come if you have a social time in connection with this meeting.

QUESTIONS FOR REVIEW

Why should care be taken in selecting officers?
What is the work of the president?
The secretary?
The treasurer?
How should a budget be made out?
What are some plans for raising money?
What is the executive committee and how should it conduct business?
Why should the society hold regular business meetings?
What is the best time for the society's business meeting?

CHAPTER VIII

SOCIETY ORGANIZATION: THE COMMITTEES

There are five committees which seem indispensable in a Junior society: the prayer-meeting, lookout, missionary, social, and sunshine committees. These should be organized as soon as possible. Of course other committees may be organized too, care being taken that every Junior, including preparatory members, is placed on some committee.

Committee meetings may be held Saturday afternoons or at any other convenient time. The superintendent and assistants will attend and will coach the chairmen beforehand. It is a good plan to appoint for each committee a secretary who will keep minutes of the committee meetings and also will keep a scrap-book in which committee plans may be pasted or written.

It is well to draw out for each committee a programme of work for the whole season. This should define the things the committee hopes to do.

Prayer-Meeting Committee.—The main duty of this committee is to plan and prepare the meetings. It should meet every two weeks and with the help of *The Junior Christian Endeavor World* and *The Christian Endeavor World* write out a programme for the two following meetings, the superintendent assisting, of course.

If questions are to be written and distributed among the members for answer in the meeting, the members of the committee will distribute them. They should also be urged to be themselves prepared to take part in the meeting and fill in pauses. It is well to choose this committee from among the older members.

Let this committee choose the design of the topic cards. Consult them on all matters relating to the meeting. Try to interest them in making each meeting slightly different from the others. Arrange the chairs differently—in a circle, in a square, in the form of the Christian Endeavor monogram; hold a leaderless meeting, the programme being written on the blackboard, or a telegram meeting, the members writing ten-word messages on the topic and reading the messages in the meeting. "Prayer-Meeting Methods," and "Fifty-two Varieties" contain suggestions for variations. A candle-light meeting, a song-writers' meeting, a motto meeting, are well-known and always enjoyed.

Gather together the committee members and the leader of the meeting for a five-minute prayer service before the meeting opens.

Let a member write on the blackboard at each meeting topics for sentence prayers as suggestions for the Juniors.

Have a question-box in the meeting room into which members may drop questions about the topic. The superintendent will reply to such questions.

This committee may also have charge of the meeting-room. In this case the members should be on hand early to arrange the chairs, to pick up hymn books that may be scattered around, to put out the society's own song books, to arrange the table and put flowers on it, and so forth.

Lookout Committee. — This committee has many duties. The first is to secure new members for the society and to plan campaigns toward this end. It is a membership committee.

Sometimes membership contests are carried out in the society, which divides its members, under the leadership of the lookout committee, into two sides, Reds and Blues, or some other name, to see which side can secure the largest number of members in a given time. Each side will be led by a captain who will guide his side and tell them what to do. When such a campaign is conducted it should be understood that all newcomers must sign as preparatory members, not as active members. As preparatory members they will attend the meeting for some time before they can be received as active members.

Another form of campaign the lookout committee may conduct is an attendance campaign, points being given to each Junior for attending the meeting himself and more points being given for his bringing a guest. It helps to give to each Junior two chairs in the meeting, placed side by side, the one chair for himself, and the other for his guest. This is a spur to all Juniors to bring guests who may be won to membership.

Such campaigns are educational. The Juniors are taught through them to plan for results. Thus the sides will make a survey of the Sunday school, writing down the names and addresses of children of Junior age who are not in the society. Names of children of proper age in the community will also be listed. The captain of each side will give to each of those under him one or two names and ask them to visit those Juniors and invite them to the meeting. Sometimes special cards of invitation will be used; at other times letters will be written.

THE COMMITTEES

But apart from special campaigns a live lookout committee will keep a permanent list of names of children in the Sunday school who are approaching Junior age. When they are old enough the committee will invite them to the meeting and keep inviting them until they come. A good way to keep in touch with such children is to have the birthday committee send them cards on their birthdays, to show that the society is interested in them.

The committee should be busy at socials. The social committee should use the lookout committee's list of names and invite these children to the socials. Then the lookout committee should give them a hearty invitation to attend the regular meeting.

This committee may get out special posters advertising the meeting. Watch the Christian Endeavor publications for new plans and do not be afraid to try them.

The superintendent will decide upon the fitness of any candidate for membership. Most children may become preparatory members, but only those that show interest should be taken as active members. When application for membership is made the name of the applicant should be presented by the chairman of the lookout committee at a regular meeting of the society and be voted upon the following meeting night.

It is as essential to keep the members we have as it is to get new ones. This is the lookout committee's duty too. When a member is absent from several meetings the committee should visit him and report the reason to the superintendent.

The lookout committee will also explain the pledge to prospective members. All the work of the committee should be done under the guidance of the superintendent.

The superintendent may use the following methods in the committee. 1. Urge the Juniors to use the telephone in inviting guests to the meetings. 2. Place posters advertising the meeting in store windows when possible. 3. Write on shipping tags an invitation to the meeting and have the Juniors tie the tags on the door knobs of houses where they know children of Junior age live. 4. . Get for the committee a visitors' book and have a member in charge of it at each meeting. Get visitors to write their names and addresses in the book; then send them a letter later telling them how glad the committee was to see them at the meeting and inviting them to come to the next meeting. 5. Sometimes the committee may have flowers on hand to give to visitors. 6. In a membership campaign draw a large wheel on cardboard. If you wish to win twenty members draw twenty spokes

THE COMMITTEES 97

on the wheel. Tell the Juniors that the plan is to find a new member for each spoke. As each new member is won write his name on a spoke.

Social Committee.—First of all, the members of the social committee should be taught to welcome strangers and be *sociable*. Teach all Juniors not to be clannish in the meetings, but show friendliness to all.

The committee plans and carries out socials. Guidance will be necessary, but the Juniors will do the work if they are told what to do. They will even contribute ideas at times. It is a fine thing to show the Juniors that a social follows a definite plan just like any other meeting. The plan will look like this:

1. *Some amusing game to mix the guests and break up formality.* (Handshaking with a paper bag tied to the right hand; names of States or cities written on slips of paper and pinned to the backs of the guests, who must guess the names they carry, and so on.)

2. *A period of fun.* Games, charades, etc.

3. *A period of instruction.* (Some one tells some facts about Christian Endeavor or the society, or gives an instructive talk on some live topic.)

4. *Refreshments.*

5. *A period of devotion*—a song service closing with prayer.

Use the great days of the calendar for socials: the Fourth of July; Lincoln's birthday; Washington's birthday; Christmas; New Year's; Easter; Valentine's Day; Hallowe'en, and so on. Many societies hold a social each month.

Get a book of socials and study the best of them. No two socials should be alike. "Good Times for Juniors" has some fine suggestions for games. So has "Successful Socials."

The work of the committee is educational, therefore the Juniors should be taught to make bright posters advertising the socials, to hand in names of guests they would like to have invited, to distribute invitations, to hand out tickets, and so forth.

Some societies object to admission charges at socials. This is a matter that must be determined by the policy of the church.

The social committee usually has charge of picnics, hikes, and so on. Assistants will be necessary on such occasions. Plan to have a definite object for each hike. In summer, for example, take along some one who knows flowers and will set the Juniors to collecting them, afterwards telling their story. On another hike some one who knows local history may take the Juniors to historical spots. On another hike take some

THE COMMITTEES 99

one who can do modelling in clay to show the Juniors how to do this interesting work.

Vary the socials. It is well to have one leading idea for each social. For instance, a shadow-picture social will make shadow pictures the main feature. One of the members of the Senior society will make shadow pictures on a sheet or on the wall, using his hands to make shadow pictures of faces, animals, and so on. Cardboard cut in the shape of a house is used effectively as a setting for some of the pictures.

A game the Juniors will enjoy is a shadow-picture guessing game. Hang a white sheet in the doorway between two rooms. Place a strong light (an electric lamp or a good lantern) on a table in one of the rooms. The Juniors will be seated in the other room. Now divide the Juniors into two sides, one-half on each side. Take one side into the room in which the table and lamp are placed. Pose five or six of the Juniors one by one between the lamp and the screen so that the shadow is clearly shown. The Juniors outside will guess the names of the Juniors whose shadows are thrown on the screen. Then change the roles of the groups, making the first set spectators and the other set actors. The side that makes the best guesses wins.

Shadow tableau can also be shown on the screen,

the spectators guessing the meaning of the pictures.

There is an endless variety of socials: a Washington's birthday social; a pin social; a singing social; an old-fashioned-games social; a charade social, and so on.

Keep the Juniors occupied all the time. They enjoy themselves best when they do not need to sit and listen too long to others performing, but can themselves take part in what is going on. Arrange for simple contests in the socials. Give the Juniors each a clothes pin and some colored paper and have a doll-dressing contest, with a small prize for the winner. Give them pieces of cardboard and ask them each to cut out of it the figure of some animal. (The names of animals should be written on slips of paper and placed in a hat; each Junior will then draw one slip and cut out the animal whose name he draws.) Dolls and animals may be made from peanuts, the Juniors using ink, toothpicks, and colored paper. Animals may be modelled in clay or plasticine.

Recreation Committee.—In small societies the social committee may act as a recreation committee; in large societies it is well to have a separate committee. This committee will keep a scrap-book of games and will be ready to help

THE COMMITTEES 101

the social committee with new games for socials. It will plan athletic drills, help to get up entertainments, form baseball and other clubs, conduct track meets for Juniors—which appeal especially to boys—organize a dramatic club to give an entertainment, arrange for a flower show, plan a kodak club, get up a pageant, and so forth.

Missionary Committee.—An assistant superintendent should have charge of the missionary committee to suggest things to do. The committee will plan the missionary meetings with the help of the assistant superintendent, who will write to the denominational missionary board, several weeks before the meeting, and ask for whatever printed material is available for the topic. This material the committee will distribute among the members, asking them to give certain facts in the meeting. The committee members will also collect missionary books bearing on the topics and assign chapters to the members to study at home.

This committee should act as a missionary-information committee and plan to give one missionary item in each meeting of the society. It will also advertise the missionary meetings well in advance.

Encourage the reading of missionary books. Have a reading contest to stimulate interest. If there are five members on the missionary committee let them challenge the whole society to a reading contest of this kind. All members of the society are to read as many missionary books and leaflets as possible. These will be secured by the superintendent either from the church library or the mission board of the denomination. *The five members of the missionary committee will undertake to read more missionary material in a given time—say one month—then the five members of the society who have read most.* Each reader will keep his own record and will hand it in each week.

The members of this committee should keep notebooks in which to write missionary items that come to them.

The committee should suggest to the society a missionary song as the society's own. A society missionary motto should also be chosen and neatly printed on cardboard to be hung in the meeting-room. The committee may collect pictures showing missionary scenes and the costumes and customs of missionary lands. These will be useful when missionary pageants or plays are presented. Occasionally have the committee call for essays on missionary topics from the members of the society.

The society should do definite missionary work —support an orphan, help to pay the salary of a native worker, support a bed in a hospital, and so on. The committee should think of home

THE COMMITTEES 103

missions and help the mountain people of the South or make up a missionary box for a missionary family, remembering especially the children.

The committee should urge a definite pledge for missions. Mite boxes may be used in the homes or in the society.

Missionary handwork is helpful. A member of the Senior society may act as instructor. The Juniors may make maps, sand maps, maps made of papier mache, sand-trays, and so on; they may construct native huts from cardboard and grass, making models of native villages. Pictures in missionary books will show what is needed. The United Society publishes a useful book on Junior handwork.

The superintendent should keep a notebook in which to write or paste plans for missionary meetings. Remember that the Juniors enjoy dramatic representation and make use of this instinct. Dyed cheesecloth makes excellent drapery for missionary costumes.

The superintendent will work out these suggestions in her missionary programme. 1. Plan meetings ahead. Get special speakers occasionally. Get the Juniors to debate various questions such as: ''Resolved, that missions are more needed in America than in India.'' Arrange for a discussion of the question: ''If I had $1,000,-

000 how should it be spent for missions?" Natives (in costume) from other lands will come in and plead for their countries; the children representing the natives, of course.

2. Put on a missionary play once every season at least.

3. Collect missionary curios and get the Juniors to help you. Use them in the meetings.

4. Organize a mission-study class. If this is impossible give a few minutes at each meeting to reading a missionary book to the Juniors.

5. Make a prayer-list for missions. Give the Juniors some facts about Africa and some missionaries there and ask them to pray for this country during the week.

6. Subscribe for a missionary periodical.

Sunshine Committee.—The motto of this committee may be "Others." Teach the Juniors to make sunshine at home by obedience and cheerfulness. The committee will take flowers to the sick and shut-ins, will visit and sing for the old and infirm, will visit old people's homes, will take dinners to the poor at Thanksgiving and Christmas, will visit sick Juniors, will each try to do a good turn every day, will cut out stories and funny sayings and place them in manila envelopes to be sent to children's hospitals. This committee also makes comfort powders, that is, slips of paper on which are written Bible texts. Seven texts are put into an envelope and the envelope is given to a convalescent person who is told to take one powder or text each day.

Flower Committee.—This committee is often combined with the sunshine committee. If these committees are separate the flower committee should work entirely with flowers: place flowers on the pulpit on Sundays; take flowers to the sick (sending with each bouquette a verse or two of Scripture written on a slip of paper, in the society's name); decorate the church in spring and fall with wild flowers or leaves; make flower mottoes for the church or meeting-room; send flower greetings to pastor, elders, and old people on their birthdays. The Juniors will enjoy a hike, arranged by the flower committee, into the country to bring flowers and leaves for church decoration. The best effect is got by massing one kind of flower: daisies, for example, in great profusion; in the fall, colored leaves; on another day, geraniums, and so forth. This committee may cultivate flowers on the church lawn, or in their homes. They may plant seeds and cuttings and give the flowers in pots to the poor or to shut-ins. The committee may offer a small prize to the Junior that brings the best flower of a certain kind to a flower-exhibition social. The committee may also take charge of the church lawn, trimming and cutting the grass when it is needed.

Birthday Committee.—This committee will keep a list of the birthdays of members of the society, of children in the Sunday school, of the pastor, members of the church board, and so forth, and will send cards of greeting to them at the proper time. The committee should write on the blackboard the names of Juniors who have birthdays in the coming week. In the society a mite-box will be kept and Juniors who have birthdays will put into it a penny for every year they are old. Birthday Juniors should be recognized in a special way. They may be asked to stand along with the society while the superintendent offers prayer for them. The committee should also have a special birthday hymn to be sung when a Junior celebrates a birthday. This may be a hymn chosen from the hymn book, or special words written to a well-known tune. Perhaps the pastor will write suitable words.

Good-Citizenship Committee.—The main work of this committee will be to work for temperance. The members will conduct temperance meetings. They will distribute among the Juniors facts about the effect of strong drink. They will read temperance magazines and give facts about the progress of prohibition in our own country and in the world. They will provide total abstinence cards

THE COMMITTEES 107

for members of the society to sign. The members of the committee should also from time to time tell temperance anecdotes to the society. They may give talks on great temperance reformers and tell the story of the fight that brought about prohibition. The committee may arrange for occasional speakers to tell the Juniors about the city government, about the police force, and about keeping and breaking the law, about clean-up campaigns, and so on.

Scrap-Book Committee.—This committee will do good work if it gets every committee in the society to keep a scrap-book in which to write or paste plans which the committee may later carry out. This is better than having the scrap-book committee make books and give them to the committee.

The committee may make scrap-books for missions. In them paste pictures only, for children in foreign lands will not understand English. Scrap-books may be made for children's hospitals. In this case stories and jokes may be pasted in them. Scrap-books may be made for the sick, or for convalescents, interesting items of news or short poems being used.

The committee may paste back to back picture postal cards and send them to missionaries on the foreign field. The denominational missionary board will provide addresses.

Music Committee.—The pianist should be chairman of this committee. Its work is to provide music in the meetings. The pianist should choose hymns at home, hymns that are suitable to the topic, and have them ready if they are needed in the meeting. Sometimes the superintendent will tell her which hymns to prepare. She should practise all the hymns in the hymn book. The committee may organize a society choir and a society orchestra. It may provide special music, solos and duets, at the meetings. It may suggest one hymn a month for the whole society to memorize. It may take charge of the society hymn books and keep them in repair. It may also conduct an occasional hymn-writers' meeting, learning the stories of some of the great hymns (there are books published that tell these stories, for instance, "A Treasure of Hymns," sold by the United Society) and telling them in the meeting before the hymns are sung.

Information Committee.—This committee's duty is to keep the society informed on the progress of Christian Endeavor. It gets its information items chiefly from *The Junior Christian Endeavor World* and *The Christian Endeavor World*. It will also tell the society of new methods of work, getting its information from the same sources or from books. It may give denominational items gleaned from the church paper, and it may tell what other Junior societies in the town are doing. To get this information two members of the committee should occasionally visit other societies.

The members of the committee will take turns, meeting about, in giving these items. If figures are used in their reports, they should use the blackboard to give them. Sometimes the information may be given in the shape of a dialogue, two members of the committee taking part. At other times the committee's report may be written in full on the blackboard. The committee may have an information bulletin, made of thick cardboard, and labeled "Information Bulletin," all to itself. On this it will paste or write information items. The bulletin will be hung in the meeting-room. Sometimes the committee will bring facts about missions, but usually this is done by the missionary committee.

Good-Literature Committee.—This committee should first of all be responsible for getting up a club of subscribers to *The Junior Christian Endeavor World*. It should also try to secure in the Senior society and the church subscribers to *The Christian Endeavor World*. It should also conduct campaigns to get all Juniors to wear the Junior Christian Endeavor pin.

Some committees collect waste paper, sell it, and give the proceeds to the society. They may conduct a literature table in the church vestibule. Many church members will give magazines for this purpose, and the Juniors will be responsible for collecting them and taking them to the church. Papers, books, and magazines may also be sent to soldiers' camps, sailors' homes, institutions, fire stations, and so on, every book and magazine being stamped with the name of the society. If the Senior society is doing this work the Junior society may co-operate with it rather than work independently. The members of the committee may read good books and in the meeting outline the story and perhaps, if the superintendent thinks it wise, read short portions.

QUESTIONS FOR REVIEW

What are the five indispensable committees?
When should committee meetings be held?
Why should committee work for the whole season be outlined?
What are the duties of the prayer-meeting committee?
The lookout committee?
What are the dangers of a membership campaign?
What are the advantages of an attendance campaign?
Name some plans to secure new members.
What steps are necessary when a child wishes to join the society?
What are the elements of a good social?
Outline work for a social committee.
What is a recreation committee?
Outline work for a missionary committee.
Outline a sunshine-committee programme.
How may the flower committee serve?
What are the duties of a birthday committee?
What work may a good-citizenship committee do?
What can Juniors do for good literature?
Describe the work of A. The scrap-book committee; B. The music committee, and C. The information committee.

CHAPTER IX

HOW TO CONDUCT A JUNIOR MEETING

The Time of Meeting.—When should a Junior society hold its meeting? The answer is, "At the time that is most convenient for the Junior superintendent and the Juniors." This time will vary according to local conditions. In rural districts it may be quite different from town or city.

A good many Junior societies meet on Sunday afternoon. Some object to this hour because it crowds the superintendent's day. Others hold their meeting Sunday morning before the church service and find this time convenient.

Many societies hold their meeting Sunday evening before the hour of the Senior gathering. A few hold the meeting during the Senior meeting hour, but this deprives the superintendent of the privilege of attending the older society's meeting.

Some societies, again, hold the meeting during the hour of morning church service. Usually the children come to church and the pastor makes a short talk to them. During the singing of a hymn the Juniors file out of the auditorium and go to their own room where they hold their meeting while the church service proceeds. This is possible, of course, only in churches that have facilities for it. Some parents like this method, for they know that the Juniors are being taken care of. The superintendent, however, loses the morning service. Some object because the Juniors also miss the morning service and the opportunity of forming the church-going habit is also lost.

Other societies have entirely given up the attempt to put the Junior meeting into Sunday at all. They have chosen a week-day afternoon or early evening. This is possible, of course, only when the superintendent is so situated that she can give this hour to the work. It makes it hard to get assistants, for most young people are at work. The objection to an evening meeting is that parents do not like to have their children out late.

After all, superintendents must consider what is the best time *for them* and their Juniors, and make arrangements accordingly. *There is no hard and fast rule about the time of meeting.*

How to Conduct a Junior Meeting.—In order to create a sense of order and discipline from the beginning some superintendents assemble the Juniors at the back of the room, or in a hallway adjoining the meeting-room, and form them in procession, two by two; while the piano plays a marching song they pass into the room singing. Usually

THE JUNIOR MEETING 113

they march around the room once or twice before filing into their places.

A good Junior meeting must be carefully prepared by the prayer-meeting committee and superintendent at least a week in advance of the meeting. The programme should be written out in advance, home work should be assigned to certain Juniors, and this fact should be noted on the programme, and the names of all Juniors who have been asked to offer prayer or otherwise take part should also be written down. If the meeting is to have real educational value this preliminary work simply must be done.

The Programme.—The programme should vary with almost every meeting. Do not fall into ruts. Study the suggestions given in the section for prayer-meeting committees; vary the arrangement of the seats, change the order of service, use the blackboard, and so forth. Make it impossible for any Junior to sit at home and imagine what the meeting will be like.

Here is a sample programme. Notice that the decision service is a distinctive feature of it. Such a service cannot be held at all times. But other features could be introduced. We do not mean that this programme should be followed at all times, even in outline. Its items may be varied, omitted, rearranged as the superintendent pleases. The programme is given merely as a sample of well-balanced work.

A Programme Suggestion.

PRE-PRAYER SERVICE. QUIET MUSIC.

I. SERVICE OF WORSHIP.
 1. Silent prayer, closed with audible prayer by the superintendent.
 2. Hymn.
 3. Responsive reading. Psalm 1.
 4. Prayer by leader.
 5. Special music.

II. FELLOWSHIP SERVICE.
 1. Welcome to new members and visitors.
 2. Prayer for absentees.
 3. Birthday greetings.

III. BIBLE DRILL.

IV. OFFERING SERVICE.
 1. Offering brought to the front.
 2. Verses on Bible giving.
 3. Offering prayer or song.

V. SERVICE OF EXPRESSION.
 1. Scripture lesson read.
 2. Daily readings discussed.
 3. Discussion of topic.
 4. Talk by superintendent.
 5. Hymn.

VI. DECISION SERVICE (in charge of pastor).

VII. CLOSING SERVICE.
 1. Consecration Hymn.
 2. Prayer and benediction.

Every programme should open with a service of

THE JUNIOR MEETING 115

worship. It will give tone to the meeting that follows if the Juniors are brought to realize that God is present with them. It is doubtful if the best way to open a Junior meeting is by singing, for the children are not usually in a worshipful mood. The silent prayer in the above programme is designed to produce this mood. Sometimes the children may pray the Lord's Prayer in unison, the superintendent leading *very slowly* (do not gallop through it), pausing distinctly between each phrase. This gives the children a chance to grasp the meaning of the words they are using. Sometimes the Juniors may be told to fold their hands, look downwards, and repeat the text. "Let the words of my mouth and the meditation of my heart be acceptable in Thy sight, O Lord, my strength and my Redeemer." Then tell them to turn their eyes to the ceiling and repeat the words, "The Lord is in his holy temple; let all the earth keep silence before him." The action accompanying these prayers is important. The attitude of worship produces the feeling of worship, just as the attitude of fear will produce the feeling of fear. William James maintains that a man runs not because he is afraid, but he is afraid because he runs. The action produces the emotion. Apply this principle to worship and seek to produce the proper emotion by appropriate action. Then the Juniors will be ready for their opening song.

The responsive reading may be conducted in various ways. The superintendent may read one verse and the Juniors the next, and so on. Or, at another time the girls may read one verse and the boys the next. The society may be divided into two halves and the two sections may read verse about. A Junior may be asked to read one verse, the society reading the responses. The society may read the passage in unison. Employ a different method each week.

In the fellowship service different Juniors may be used for the three things specified. Their tasks should be assigned to them at least a week before the meeting.

There are two parts to the Bible drill. First there is drill proper, giving the names of Bible books, and finding passages in the Bible. Then there is Bible memory work. Give time to each part.

In the service of expression no mention is made of a blackboard-talk or an object-talk. Use these when you can. Let the Juniors show the objects and give the talks; also let them draw the pictures on the blackboard.

Sentence prayers may also be made a part of the service of expression. Teach the Juniors that a sentence prayer means what it says, just a *sentence*. The week before the meeting the prayer-meeting committee may give to some Juniors slips of paper

THE JUNIOR MEETING 117

with the words written on them, "*Sentence Prayers for* ...." Write in the topic, such as for "Help to do our duty"; "For the church"; "For the Society"; "For the pastor." The topic for the day will suggest subjects for sentence prayers.

Or again, these subjects for prayer may be written on the blackboard. The Juniors should also be taught to memorize Bible prayers and offer them when suitable. Examples will be found in the chapter on Bible Drills and memory work.

Accustom the Juniors to pray in public, to express simply their wants and aspirations and not merely to imitate the prayers of the pastor or of grown-ups. Encourage them even to write out their little prayers, memorize them, and offer them in the meeting.

The superintendent should sit beside the leader at the table in front of the society, but the leader should be expected really to lead the meeting. The superintendent will give a short talk, perhaps tell a story on the topic. She should also try to have a story-illustration for a Junior to give. But she should not monopolize the time. Her aim should be to get the Juniors to take part. This may be difficult at first, and when they get started their efforts will be crude; but they will gain confidence and as time passes will learn to express themselves more than creditably. They have not yet reached the age of diffidence and self-criticism. They are natural in what they do.

The society must not be turned into a Sunday school class. The more the Juniors do for themselves the better is the society doing its work.

The programme which we have just cited does not give handwork a place. Usually there will not be time in the meeting for the Juniors to do much if any handwork; but if the superintendent, with the help of an assistant, can hold a handwork class on a week afternoon or evening and get the Juniors to cut out objects in paper or cardboard, or model them in clay, or make models of scenes (using the sand-tray) referred to in the lesson, it will help to show these objects in the meeting and build up the story around them. In missionary meetings such handwork is indispensable; in connection with Bible topics that refer to scenes that can be presented in rude model, it is a fine help. Bottle dolls or cardboard dolls represent the characters in Bible story. But see the book, "Handwork for Juniors" for particulars.

Many Junior societies make a custom of studying a missionary book each season. The society becomes a mission-study class part of the time, the superintendent reading, telling, or explaining the story. In such a case handwork is a splendid aid, for the various scenes can be built up in *papier mache* or on a sand tray; the country can be represented with rivers, lakes, and sea; villages can be made out of raffia and grass; and dolls, properly costumed, represent the people.

Missionary magazines contain so much fine material that there will be no difficulty in building up a good programme. Juniors readily personify the natives. They are at the age when they try on other people's experience, and they will thoroughly enter into the spirit of foreign life and express it in their own way, if they are allowed to act out missionary scenes.

Pageants.—Juniors are always enthusiastic about putting on a missionary pageant or play. The mission boards are ready to supply good ones. As we have already pointed out, dyed cheesecloth makes excellent costume material. In the same way, Juniors eagerly act out Bible stories, speaking the parts of the characters. Such dramatic expression makes a deep mark on the minds of children.

Repetition and Enforcement.—Usually the Junior topic contains one outstanding thought. In preparing the programme the superintendent should have this thought clearly in mind. She should ask herself the questions before she begins, "What is the main thought in this topic which I wish to enforce? What response do I wish to get?" She should write down the answers to these really vital questions and shape her method to get results.

The first thing to remember is that repetition

counts. The leading thought, the principal truth, should be repeated again and again in various ways. It will be found in the leader's talk, in the illustration or story given by the superintendent, and it will come out in some of the talks by the Juniors. This repetition forces the truth into the minds of the Juniors.

This clear-cut presentation of truth wins response. Every worth-while topic for Juniors can be so taught as to bring out some duty that the Juniors may perform during the week. Always try to dig a channel in the children's minds for expression in some act. Connect, if you can, the truth taught with something that the child can do in daily life. If the topic cannot thus be made practical it is not a good one for a Junior meeting. Never forget the application. Show how truth should issue in deeds; create if possible enthusiasm to go forth and do the things about which the society has been talking.

Remember that the approach to a child's interest is through things that he knows in daily experience. Truth cannot be taught in a vacuum. It must be hung on to some knowledge that the child has before. When you talk to Juniors think of the things that you know Juniors know, and work such things into illustrations, making them the starting-point for any impression you wish to produce.

THE JUNIOR MEETING

The Consecration Meeting.—Juniors should be taught that they really renew their pledge in every consecration meeting. When they stand up and repeat it in unison, seek to make this a true act of worship.

The roll-call also differentiates the consecration meeting from an ordinary meeting. Many societies find it helpful if they make this a test of the way in which the Juniors have kept the pledge during the month. Indeed some societies have found the method so helpful that they call the roll every week.

In such cases the Juniors are expected to do two things every day—to pray and read some part of the Bible, as the pledge demands. At roll-call, if a Junior has done both every day in the week, he answers "Faithful" when his name is called. If he has omitted one or two days he answers "Partly." But if he has missed three days or more in the week he answers "Failed." If the roll is called monthly only two responses should be asked for: "Faithful" from those that have not missed a day; and "Partly" from those that have missed one day or more.

Vary the roll-call. The booklet "Our Crowning Meeting" gives many methods of doing this. As samples we may mention the following:

Write the names of the Juniors on cards; arrange the cards in alphabetical order, according to the last names of the Juniors, and call the names in this order. Another time arrange the names in alphabetical order, but use the *first* names of the Juniors in doing so. Another Sunday arrange the names of the members in the order of the streets in which they live. Again, mix the cards and call the names as they fall. Once more, give to each Junior as he comes into the room a number and call the names in the order of the numbers. The secretary who gives the numbers will of course keep a record of the names of the Juniors to whom they are given.

At the consecration meeting especially, but for that matter in all meetings, the superintendent should make much of sentence prayers. Encourage the Juniors to write sentence prayers at home, memorize them, and give them in the meeting.

QUESTIONS FOR REVIEW

When should a Junior society hold its meetings?
How may we create a sense of decorum at the beginning of a meeting?
Who prepares the programme of the Junior meeting?
How may we vary the programme of the Junior meeting?
Outline a programme for a Junior meeting.
What are the elements of a Junior programme?
What are Bible drills? How conduct them?
How can we teach Juniors to pray in public?
What value has handwork in a Junior meeting?
How may we arrange Junior pageants?
How may we enforce a lesson by repetition?
How may we secure the child's interest?
Describe different ways of calling the roll.

CHAPTER X

WORK THE SOCIETY MAY DO

A good deal of the work which the committees regularly do must be done during the week, and thus the committee system provides for through-the-week activities. Besides this work, however, the society as a group, and members as individuals, may do many things. The following is a list of suggestions taken from actual work done by societies. The superintendent should choose carefully the tasks she wishes the society to perform. It is a good plan to make a list of them and announce to the Juniors at the beginning of the season what they are. They may be printed on a large piece of cardboard and hung in front of the society so that no one may forget them.

Sometimes some of these tasks will naturally fall under the work of a committee. For instance, if the society decides to support an orphan in a missionary home, the missionary committee will be especially interested in this, and the committee may be given charge of collecting funds and making reports. So with much of the other work.

No society will attempt to do all these things at once. Take the easiest first and gradually add others. Do not be in a hurry to accomplish everything. The following list makes no pretence of being complete. Superintendents will be able to think of other work that is needed in their locality and will doubtless do it.

But just to show what a live Junior society can do, here is a report of things done in one year in a Junior society:

Juniors joined the Red Cross.

Juniors took courses in first aid and surgical dressing.

Juniors knitted for the Red Cross.

Juniors sold war-saving stamps.

Juniors sold Liberty Bonds.

Juniors wrote letters to soldiers.

Juniors bought a $100 government bond.

Juniors held a bazaar which netted a profit of $30.

Juniors started a fund to buy furniture for the Junior and Sunday-school room.

Juniors gave eight baskets of food at Christmas to poor families.

Juniors made eight mistletoe wreaths at Christmas for the poor.

Juniors bought and sent a large box of candy to the poor farm.

Juniors visited nineteen shut-ins during the holidays.

Juniors held serenades for shut-ins.

Juniors gave a Christmas gift of $19 to the orphans' home.

Juniors held eight socials.

Juniors made scrap-books for the different committees.

Flower committee grew bulbs, sold some, and gave others for church decoration.

Juniors conducted a mission-study class.

This is a really fine amount of work done. No doubt other societies are doing as well. The following are a few more hints for things to do:

Help a church-attendance campaign by distributing invitations and so on.

Make money for the society by selling photographs, cards, magazines, and other articles.

Conduct a reading-circle and report to the society on books read.

Organize a flower-day for the church.

Buy a phonograph for a children's hospital, the poor farm, or other institution.

Place *The Christian Endeavor World* in the public library.

Hold a class in Expert Endeavor, using "The Junior Text-Book."

Start a fund to buy a complete Junior Christian Endeavor library for the use of the society.

Start a fund to buy a missionary library. Also try to get church members to donate books toward this library.

Buy athletic equipment, baseballs and bats, for the boys.

Conduct a magazine table in the church vestibule; collect from church members the magazines for, it and place them on the table.

If a country society, invite a certain number of Juniors from some poor section of the city for a day in the country. Feed them well and give them a good time.

Help the Gideons to place Bibles in the hotels of your town.

Attend Christian Endeavor rallies in a body.

Try to organize new societies, visiting churches where there are no societies, and holding model meetings to interest the Juniors there.

Visit orphans' homes, old people's homes, and other institutions.

Give Thanksgiving baskets to the poor.

Be Santa Claus to several poor children.

Occasionally give a demonstration of Junior work, especially memory work, in the Sunday-evening church service, if the pastor desires it.

Supply *The Christian Endeavor World* and other magazines to railroad depot and barber shops.

WORK THE SOCIETY MAY DO

Put in the guest boxes at hotels invitations to attend the church services on Sunday.

Write letters to absent members.

Support a native worker in a mission land.

Take a dime and trade with it all summer, giving the profit to the society.

Once in a while attend in a body the church's midweek service. The pastor will probably permit the Juniors to take some part in the service.

Arrange hikes, marshmallow roasts, athletic meets, and so on..

Give to the superintendent the names and addresses of all children who move into your street or district.

Give to the pastor the names of new families that move into the district.

Hold a Christmas tree for the children of your district.

Give entertainments.

Conduct an every-member canvass to secure pledges to mission work.

Prepare scrap-books and postal cards for missionaries.

Secure and send to missionaries (write your board for addresses) pictures that have been used in the Sunday school.

Start a society stamp book; the Juniors to collect stamps that may be sold, the profits to go to the society's treasury.

Hold sewing classes for girls.

Start a boys' club. Invite the boys of the district.

Work in clean-up campaigns in spring.

Conduct a booth at a church fair.

Buy and erect in front of the church, with the pastor's consent, a "Silent Preacher," or bulletin board on which messages are posted from time to time.

Organize a Junior choir and orchestra.

Write individual letters of greeting to church officers and pastor on their birthdays.

Celebrate "Arbor Day."

Plan a surprise for the pastor.

Present to the church a pulpit Bible.

Buy carpet for some room in church which needs it.

Pay the church electric-light bill, or part of it.

Help to pay the coal bill.

Present to old ladies' home a box of quilt patches.

Hold a potato meeting, the members each bringing several potatoes, which are given to the poor after the meeting. One society planted the potatoes and gave the crop to the poor.

Cultivate a society garden and give the produce to the poor.

Raise money to put a stained glass window in the church.

WORK THE SOCIETY MAY DO 129

Tighten bolts on the seats in the meeting room.

Repair damaged or worn cushions in church (this is work for girls).

Paste covers on hymn books if they are detached.

Buy a society rubber stamp and stamp all hymn books and magazines.

Have a clean-up night when the members get out all books, hymn books, Bibles, and so on, and rub out all pencil marks, besides repairing books that need repair.

If the society's badges or sashes get frayed the girls may have a sewing bee and repair them.

Keep the church lawn tidy. Tend flowers around the church.

Make a collection of missionary curios or objects from mission lands.

Make a collection of missionary pictures, pasting them on cardboard or in a special scrap-book. Paste in or write the story of each picture.

Support or help to equip a kindergarten for foreign children.

Hold a gift service at Christmas, the gifts to go to the poor.

Get names from United Charities or other organization and have Juniors mail their magazines and papers to other children.

Help to pay rent of a poor family.

Help Christian Endeavor fresh-air homes which

give poor children a two-weeks vacation in the country.

Help the State and local Christian Endeavor unions.

Help world-wide Christian Endeavor through the United Society of Christian Endeavor.

Buy and send to a mission field a mirrorscope for throwing picture postal cards on a large screen.

Some missions need baby organs, clarinets, money to dig a well, patch-work pieces of goods, bags in which candy may be placed at Christmas. Such things the Junior society may procure and send.

QUESTIONS FOR REVIEW

Outline a season's work for a Junior society.
Write out from memory a list of things a Junior society may do.
How can we interest the whole society in its programme of work?

CHAPTER XI

JUNIOR EDUCATIONAL PROGRAMME

Material has been given in the foregoing chapters for an educational programme for Juniors. It covers the physical life, the mental life, the moral and the spiritual life.

1. THE BODY. The Junior society does not profess to be a school of athletics. It merely makes use of the fact that the body of the Junior is developing and craves activity, and attempts to use this activity in order to teach moral and spiritual truths. Of course Junior superintendents are interested in the health of Juniors, and it is quite within their province, if need be, to give them health instruction. But this is the work rather of other institutions and while Christian Endeavor must sympathize with it and help it as occasion demands, it cannot give much time to it, except in the indirect way of hikes and outings.

2. THE MIND. The three mental activities with which we have to do are thought, feeling, and

will. How does Christian Endeavor propose to develop them?

A. *Thought.* For the development of thought in its religious significance Christian Endeavor provides Bible drills, Bible memory work, and independent thinking. Juniors are called upon to take part in the meeting; they are not only expected to prepare for this at home, but questions are given them to answer, topics are given them to develop, and in the meeting they are expected to express whatever thoughts they may have achieved.

B. *Feeling.* The aim of Christian Endeavor is to produce in the child's mind a definite emotional attitude toward the truths studied in the society. For example, a study of the parable of the Good Samaritan will do more than enlighten the mind; it should produce a definite emotion, a feeling of the nobility of the Samaritan's act, and at the same time a desire to emulate it. Feeling is the driving force of will and it is therefore necessary in any educational programme whatever that is to relate itself to life, to stir the emotions that the will may act.

Both instinct and habit have their roots in feeling and draw their sustenance from that source. Thus if in our meetings we can produce the right attitude of Juniors toward moral and spiritual truths we shall establish them in righteousness.

C. *Will.* Will is simply thought and feeling brought to the point of action. We must beware lest we let our topics spread out and disappear like water lost in sand. Every topic should issue in action and for this the will must be moved to decide. The Juniors should be led to make the application themselves if possible and to say, perhaps silently, "I will do this," or "I will be like that." Sometimes the superintendent will be able to suggest appropriate action that the Juniors may take during the week. For instance, after a story like that of the good Samaritan, or a study of Matt. 25, "Inasmuch as ye have done it unto the least of these my brethren, ye have done it unto me," she may suggest doing something for some poor person: taking flowers to them, sending them a basket of food, or some candy. The extent of the service is not so important as that some service be done as an expression of the lesson learned.

3. THE SOUL. Religious training includes Bible knowledge and moral instruction, but it goes beyond these things and enters into deeper relations. The soul craves God. Even children may be led to accept Christ as Saviour, Friend, and Master, and follow Him. Even children may experience God in their lives and learn to love Him, obey Him, and pray to Him as to a Friend. Junior

Christian Endeavor aims at these high ends. The prayer meeting provides an opportunity for worship. The Quiet Hour provides the same opportunity in private. Bible memory work feeds the soul. The superintendent is in reality an evangelist, and her constant aim should be to lead the Juniors definitely to yield their hearts and lives to Christ.

Missionary Education.—The suggestions already given for missionary meetings and work in committees provide no mean missionary education. The great thing is to interest Juniors in missions. That Junior Christian Endeavor is doing this is seen when Juniors enter Intermediate or Senior society and from it go, and many of them do, to the mission field. It is well to begin early to give children the world outlook. The world must be redeemed by the men of to-morrow. Junior Christian Endeavor puts missionary interest into the society and each season has one missionary textbook for study, and sometimes two.

Co-ordinate the Work.—The programme of work for children in the church should be co-ordinated so that it does not seriously overlap. This seems obvious, yet the fact is that in many churches we find the Sunday school, the Junior society, and possibly other organizations doing in part the same kind of work.

Look at this matter from the standpoint of the Junior. In the Sunday school, let us say, he is given home memory work to do. He joins the Junior society and there he is also given home memory work to do. He may be a member of a mission band, and it may also set him home memory tasks. There is unnecessary overlapping in a case like this. But the same is true of other features, such as missions.

The cure for this situation is a Junior-work council in the church. The head of every department of Junior work in the church should be a member of this council. The council should meet under the chairmanship of the pastor and discuss the whole programme of work for children. Definite parts should be assigned to each organization and in this way the children's training will be rounded into a perfect whole.

This does not mean, of course, that the Sunday school must not mention missions, but that it should not specialize on them. Let another organization do that. If in a church a mission band is giving to the children of Junior age (7 to 13) adequate missionary training, covering the ground in mission-study classes, reading books, arranging pageants, and so on, then the Junior society need not emphasize this side of the work, but give its energies to some other. In many cases it will be found that even where a mission band exists it cannot do all the expressional missionary work needed, and such work, clearly defined, may be assigned to the society to do.

The principle to follow is to assign the work among the societies or organizations that can do it best; specifying the emphasis which each organization shall put on each subject, and thus avoid all needless duplication. Junior superintendents will be happy to co-operate in such a plan and may even take steps to put it into operation.

The Child's Quiet Hour.—Juniors are more than ready to sign a Quiet Hour covenant, just like grown-ups. They need not give so much time to their Quiet Hour as older people, but they can read the Bible every day and pray daily to God. This is all that the Quiet Hour demands of them. The covenant reads:

COVENANT CARD
of the
COMRADES OF THE JUNIOR QUIET HOUR

TRUSTING in the Lord Jesus Christ for strength, I will make it the rule of my life to set apart at least five minutes every day, if possible in the early morning, for prayer and Bible reading.

Signed..

Date..

To join the Junior Quiet Hour all that is necessary is for the Junior to sign this covenant (cards may be gotten from the United Society of the Christian Endeavor), keep it, and send the name to the Secretary, United Society of Christian Endeavor, 41 Mt. Vernon Street, Boston, Mass.

The superintendent should instruct all who sign this covenant how to keep the Quiet Hour. And by the way, she should herself keep the Quiet Hour or she will hardly be able to teach others. She should tell the Juniors always to pray, however briefly, when they rise in the morning. If they have time they may read the Bible then too; but if not, then they may read it some time during the day or at night.

This is the essence of keeping the covenant, but the Juniors may be told of other things to do. They should read the "Daily Portion," or daily Bible reading connected with the topic for the week. (Booklets with daily readings are printed and should be used by every Junior. A very helpful book is "The Child's Quiet Hour," by Mrs. Francis E. Clark.) They may keep a notebook and write down any thought that comes to them while they read; and such thoughts may be given in the meeting. In many homes the children may ask their parents the meaning of difficult passages.

A more difficult matter is to instruct the children how to pray. The superintendent should tell them that God hears prayer, silent as well as oral. He is always present with us, although unseen, and loves us like a father. Tell the Juniors to imagine Him their Father and just talk to Him as they would talk to their own father. Tell them that they may speak to God about anything whatever, but that they may not get all they ask for. God is wise and will not give us foolish things, or things that will harm us. But things that we know He wants us to have we may believe we shall get sooner or later. Thus if we ask Him to help us resist temptation, He will do it if we trust Him.

Some Juniors may be told to memorize hymns as a part of their Quiet Hour. The aim is devotional and should be kept so. Do not make it a part of memory work alone.

The Tenth Legion.—The Tenth Legion is an enrollment of those that promise to give one-tenth of their income to the Lord's work. The income of Juniors is small, but they can be taught to give one-tenth of it, whatever it be, to God. The habit of tithing acquired in childhood is easily maintained throughout life. It is a good habit for the church, but it is a better one for the individual who acquires it. It teaches Him that God is a partner in his life; it broadens the individual's sympathies; it gives him money enough as a rule

JUNIOR EDUCATIONAL PROGRAM

to help those that need help.

To join the Tenth Legion Juniors may write and sign a simple promise to give one-tenth of their income to the Lord's work, then, through the superintendent, send their names to the General Secretary of the United Society of Christian Endeavor, 41 Mt. Vernon Street, Boston, Mass.

The superintendent will tell the Juniors about God's command to the Jews to give a tenth, just as they were commanded to set apart one day in the week for religious purposes. In a sense the tithe is to our money what Sunday is to our time. God demands one-seventh of our time and at least one-tenth of our money.

Suggest that Junior Tenth Legioners keep an account with God. They may use a small book. In one column they will write down all money received or earned. Divide it by ten each week and set down this amount in another column. This is the tenth, or the Lord's portion, and should be set apart for His work.

Money, however, given to the Juniors by parents or friends for church or Sunday school collections should be given for this purpose and not counted as income. Income is only what one gets for himself alone.

The Juniors should decide how they will spend this tenth. It is God's and must of course go to His work; but they must determine to what phase of that work it shall go, whether to missions, or to church, or to the poor; or what portions shall go to these causes.

This puts responsibility on the Junior and teaches him how to handle his money. It is only a step from this administration of money to the administration of time and of life itself. The parables of stewardship will take on new meaning when they are studied and the foundations of a life of stewardship will be laid in the minds of the children.

A Society Educational Policy.

A policy contains selected items of work to be done in the coming year. It will touch all the *kinds* of work that Juniors should do, but will not attempt to put everything possible into the list. The items should be listed and printed on a large sheet of paper to hang in front of the society. The following is simply a sample and should not be followed slavishly.

I. TRAINING IN THE THEORY OF CHRISTIAN ENDEAVOR

A class in "The Junior Text-Book."
Every Junior reading the Junior leaflet that deals with his work.

II. TRAINING LEADERS

  A. Hold regular executive-committee meetings.
  B. Hold regular business meetings for the society.
  C. Have a finance committee to help the treasurer.
  D. Every Junior leading at least one meeting.

III. TRAINING IN SERVICE

  A. Committees organized: for instance, the prayer-meeting, lookout, missionary, social, and sunshine and flower. Other committees if possible.
  B. A definite plan for committee work each month for each committee.
  C. Every Junior a member of some committee.
  D. To study missions and do definite missionary work.
  E. To do something to help the poor and the sick.
  F. (Insert items of work such as are suggested in the chapter "Work a Junior Society May Do.")

IV. SPIRITUAL TRAINING

 A. Active membership attending the church service.
 B. Preparation by every Junior at home for the Junior meeting.
 C. Participation by every Junior in the Junior meeting.
 D. Doing regular memory work.
 E. Every Junior a Comrade of the Child's Quiet Hour.
 F. At least one-half of the Juniors members of the Tenth Legion.
 G. Society studies, denominational history or catechism.
 H. Memorize a hymn each month.
 I. Read a book of the Bible each month.

The above is very general. The superintendent should insert particulars. For instance, she should specify the missions or missionary book to be studied; the work the society will do for others; the memory work to be accomplished; the memory hymns to be learned; and the book of the Bible to be read each month.

Graduation.—At the age of thirteen, generally speaking, Juniors may be graduated into the Intermediate society, or, if there is no Intermediate society, into the Senior. This age is not fixed, however, since some children mature earlier and some later than others. Some may be ready for graduation at twelve; some may go on until they are fourteen. The superintendent should study the child and determine the time of graduation.

Graduation Requirements.—Some societies require those Juniors who graduate to do a certain amount of preparatory work, principally memory work. The standard must be determined by the superintendent. For instance the Juniors may be required to study the Junior efficiency leaflets or the book, "The Junior Text-Book," to give them a clear idea of the theory and methods of Christian Endeavor. They should be able to repeat several hymns from memory; to have read certain portions of the Bible (which the superintendent will select); and to have done a definite amount of Bible memory work.

A Graduation Standard.—This is merely a suggestion. Superintendents may make their own standards:
1. Memorize at least ten of the "Practical Passages." (See Chapter XII.)
2. Must have a good record of attendance (the superintendent to decide).

3. Must have studied at least four of the Junior Efficiency leaflets.
4. Must have led a meeting.
5. Must have served in all at least six months as an officer.
6. Must have served on two committees.
7. Memorize at least six hymns.
8. Must have read a missionary book selected by superintendent.
9. Must have done some handwork, made a scrap-book, a poster, or sunshine article to be given to poor children.

Graduation Exercises.—It is best to graduate Juniors in groups and a good time is Christian Endeavor Day, although any other time will do as well. Some societies hold graduation exercises on the last day on which the graduating Juniors are to be with the Junior society. Other societies plan to have a joint meeting with the Intermediate or Senior society, as the case may be, when the Juniors are graduated. In any case a special exercise should be prepared. This will include singing of a graduation song, a graduation prayer, short talks by the president of the Junior society and of the Intermediate society, and perhaps the graduating Juniors may take some part in the meeting. They will sign the pledge of the older society, and this should be made a feature and the occasion of a short talk of welcome to them by the pastor. The United Society of Christian Endeavor has a graduation exercise for Juniors which may prove useful.

It is a fine practice for a Junior society to present to each graduating Junior a Christian Endeavor pin and exhort him or her to wear it.

The interest of the superintendent in the Juniors should not cease when they graduate. She may do much to help them to feel themselves at home in the older society, especially if she herself is a member of it. She should see that they are placed on some committee; she should tell the president of the society something about each Junior's qualifications; and she should try to help the graduate Juniors to take some part in the older society's meetings. They must be encouraged lest they fall into silence and lose interest. The transition must be made as easy for them as possible, and it should be the aim of the lookout committee of the older society to lead the graduates into the society's life. It would be a good idea if societies had a *welcoming committee* whose duty it would be especially to make newcomers, graduates and others, welcome, introduce them to others, try to build up friendships, and secure invitations for new members to the homes of some of the old.

QUESTIONS FOR REVIEW

How may the society help develop the bodies of Juniors?
How does Christian Endeavor train Juniors to think for themselves?
How can we guide a child's emotional life?
What is will and how should we appeal to it?
What should be the aim of religious training in the society?
How can we teach missions to Juniors?
Why should the work of all Junior organizations in a church be co-ordinated, and how can this be done?
What is the Child's Quiet Hour, and how join it?
What may Juniors do in their Quiet Hour?
What is the Tenth Legion?
What should Juniors be taught about giving?
Outline a society educational policy.
When should Juniors be graduated?
Outline some standards of graduation.
How should graduation exercises be conducted?

CHAPTER XII

BIBLE DRILLS AND MEMORY WORK

Bible Drills.—The object of Bible drills is to accustom Juniors to use their Bibles. The drill is mechanical, not spiritual, but it nevertheless helps the Juniors in later years when they take up a more careful study of the Book than they can pursue as children.

Learning the Names of the Bible Books.—This is the first step. How should it be done? Let the superintendent write out a scheme like this:

OLD TESTAMENT

1. *The Books of Moses*: Genesis, Exodus, Leviticus, Numbers, Deuteronomy.
2. *The Historical Books*: Joshua to Esther.
3. *The Poetical Books*: Job, Psalms, Proverbs, Ecclesiastes, Song of Solomon.
4. *The Great Prophets*: Isaiah, Jeremiah, Ezekiel, Daniel.
5. *The Lesser Prophets*: Hosea to Malachi.

New Testament

1. *The Four Gospels*: Matthew, Mark, Luke, John.
2. *History of the Church*: Acts.
3. *Paul's Letters*: Romans to Philemon.
4. *Other Letters*: Hebrews to Jude.
5. *Prophecy*: Revelation.

For the Old Testament get five fairly large pieces of cardboard or stiff paper. On one write "The Books of Moses," following this with the names of the books. On another write "The Historical Books," writing the name of each book in full. Give a card to each section, and do the same with the New Testament.

Get the Juniors to copy the first card and memorize the names. The second week show them the second card, get them to copy it, and memorize the names. In this way go through all sections; but do not hurry. Give the Juniors time to do the work thoroughly. Keep reviewing the work of past weeks. Only through persistent repetition will the Juniors absorb these names and their relations.

It may help them, after they have mastered the names, let us say, of the Old Testament books, and the cards are hung in order on the wall, if the superintendent relates the groups to one another by

BIBLE DRILLS—MEMORY WORK 149

outlining very briefly the Bible story in this fashion:

i. *Genesis* is the book of beginnings: it tells us about creation, or the beginning of the world, the beginning of sin, of agriculture, of art, of industry, of God's choosing Abraham and his family.

Exodus shows us Abraham's descendants in slavery in Egypt and tells how God redeems them and brings them out of bondage.

Leviticus is a book of laws.

Numbers tells the story of Israel's wandering from Egypt to Canaan.

Deuteronomy is a summary of the law told in great speeches.

ii. *The Historical Books* tell how Israel entered Canaan and conquered the land (*Joshua*); how they lived there under judges (*Judges*); *Ruth* is a beautiful story of those days of the Judges; the books of *Samuel* (who was the last of the Judges) tell how Israel set up a kingdom under Saul and later under David; while the books of *Kings* and *Chronicles* tell the history of the kingdom—how in the days of the son of Solomon the twelve tribes quarreled and ten tribes, ever after called Israel, separated from the other two, called Judah. These books tell of the reigns of the kings in both kingdoms and of how, because of sin, Israel was overcome by enemies and carried away captive from their land, never to return. Years later Judah was also conquered and carried to Babylon, but after more than half a century, in the days of *Ezra* and *Nehemiah,* Judah returned to Palestine and built the temple and the city of Jerusalem. *Esther* is a story of what happened to some Jews in Babylon.

If the Juniors once catch *the sequence of events* they will always know where to look for these books.

In the same way relate the Great Prophets to this history. *Isaiah* lived *before* the captivity. *Jeremiah* lived immediately before it and took part in the events that led up to it. *Ezekiel* was one of those who was carried to Babylon and prophesied there. *Daniel* grew up in Babylon and prophesied there.

The other prophets are harder to place and may be left for later study.

Drill in Finding Books.—While the Juniors are learning the names and sequence of these books test them each Sunday in finding the books rapidly. Name a book and have the Juniors search for it; the one that finds it first should rise. Book-finding contests are helpful.

The New Testament.—Teach the names of the books in the same way and point out *the sequence*— the story of Jesus in the gospels; the story of the church in Acts; instruction in life and Christian teaching in the letters; and prophecy in Revelation.

A Card Drill.—Prepare cards about 2 inches broad and 4 inches long. Punch a small hole at one end of each card so that the card may be hung on a nail.

Now write the names of the books of the Bible on the cards, one name on each card. Shuffle the cards and let the Juniors arrange them in proper order. If you can have nails on the wall on which to hang the cards this will enable the Juniors to follow the one who is rearranging the names; but if not, arrange them on a table.

A contest on speed of rearrangement may be held; two Juniors may take part on each side and work together. If you have only one set of cards the sides should be carefully timed.

Verse-Finding Drill.—After the Juniors have learned the names and places of the books of the Bible a few minutes may be given at every meeting for verse-finding drills. Children attain remarkable proficiency and speed at this work, which should be kept up during the society's life.

The superintendent, an assistant, or one of the Juniors may give out the verses for which the Juniors are to search. The proper method of doing this in a drill is to keep to the last the vital point, namely, the name of the book. If the passage to be searched for is Isaiah 40:10, the superintendent will say, "Chapter 40, verse 10." Pause a moment to let all the Juniors get this clearly, then name the book, "Isaiah," and the pack is off at once.

Verse-finding contests may be held between Reds and Blues, the society being divided into two groups for this purpose; or contests between committees; or a verse-finding bee may be held at a social, two sides participating, points being given to the side finding each verse first, and the side winning which has the largest number of points. A straight verse-finding spell-down may be held, one point being given to each Junior who finds a verse first, the Junior winning who makes the highest score.

Spelling Drill.—The Juniors should be taught to spell the names of the Bible books correctly. A spell-down, using only words that appear in the few moments may be given to spelling the names at each meeting.

A variation may be made in this way. Ask the Juniors to read a book in the Bible, say Ruth or James or First John. Then at a social have a book agreed upon. The Junior wins who keeps going longest.

Combination Drill and Memory Work.—To keep Bible texts fresh in the memory of the Juniors the

BIBLE DRILLS—MEMORY WORK 153

superintendent may write out catch phrases from a number of texts and test the Juniors with them. Thus, she will say, "God so loved.." If a Junior remembers the whole text he may rise and repeat it.

Insist on the Juniors' not only repeating the texts—all texts—but also giving chapter and verse for them. This will prove valuable later.

A Parable Drill.—When the Juniors have mastered the parables of Jesus, drill them by having them tell the parable story and its application. One parable may be enough for each meeting, two at the most. The other Juniors will benefit by this drill, and the parables will be fixed in the minds of those that have studied them.

Do the same thing with the miracles of Jesus.

Map Drills.—The Sunday school probably has a wall map of Palestine, and the society may get permission to use it. If there is no such map, the society may earn money and buy one. There are several kinds of maps: first of all, the ordinary flat map with names of places. This is good, if it is the best that you can get. Use it and drill the Juniors in finding the principal places in Bible story in it: Jerusalem; Galilee; Judea; Gennesaret, and so on.

One thing is important: connect events with the places. A mere name has no interest to Juniors, but if events are linked up with the names, both the events and the names will stand clearly forth in their memories. Thus Gennesaret should always be connected with the draft of fishes (Luke 5:1), and other events; Jerusalem with the crucifixion, the cleansing of the temple, and so forth. In the map drill, therefore, the Juniors will not only find the towns, but also tell what happened there.

A better map than the flat map is one that gives a bird's eye view of the country and shows towns and mountain ranges. Such a map may be used to great profit. It may be used also for the Juniors to copy in *papier mache* (see "Handwork for Juniors" for method). This will give the children a far better idea of the country than a flat map can do.

Map-drill, of course, can be applied to mission countries, and the Junior will find the mission stations and tell their stories.

Bible-Biography Drill.—The superintendent or one of the older Juniors tells the story of some Bible character, without mentioning the name, and the Juniors guess who is referred to. Sometimes only part of the story is told and the Juniors supplement it with other facts.

BIBLE ALPHABETS.

The usual way to build up a Bible Alphabet is by asking the Juniors the first Sunday to bring to the next meeting a Bible verse beginning with the letter "A." Each Junior will read or recite his verse in the meeting, and the society, guided by the superintendent, will select the best verse quoted. All the members will then make a note of this verse and memorize it for the following meeting. The superintendent will write the letter "A" followed by the chosen verse on a large sheet of paper hung on the wall.

The second week the Juniors are asked to bring verses beginning with "B," and the best verse is selected. In this way go through the alphabet. The superintendent, of course, will have a verse ready each week in case the Juniors have not found any.

A good plan is to divide the society into two sides and have an alphabet contest. Each side scores ten points when its verse is selected—the superintendent being judge—the other side scoring five points when it has a good verse which, however, is not considered the best.

A Great-Word Alphabet.—Here is an alphabet built upon another principle—great words in the Bible. Ask the Juniors to memorize these verses, one or two—perhaps more than that—each week.

This alphabet is merely a suggestion of what may be done along this line. The superintendent will easily build up others, using other words and finding the texts by means of a concordance. In this case the word "Abide" has been chosen, but "abstain" or "ashamed" or "ask" or many other words would have done as well.

A bide—John 15:7.
B read—John 6:35.
C ontentment—1 Tim. 6:6.
D eath—John 8:51.
E ternal Life—Rom. 6:23.
F orgiveness—Eph. 1:7.
G race—Eph. 2:8.
H oliness—2 Cor. 7:1.
I nheritance—1 Pet. 1:3, 4.
J oy—John 15:11.
K ingdom—Rom. 14:17.
L ove—John 14:15.
M ercy—Jas. 5:11.
N eighbor—Rom. 15:2.
O bedience—Heb. 5:8.
P eace—Phil. 4:7.
Q uietness—2 Thess. 3:11.
R ighteousness—Matt. 6:33.
S alvation—Heb. 2:3.
T idings—Luke 2:10.
U nderstanding—Prov. 2:2, 3.

V engeance—Rom. 12:19.
W ork—John 9:4.
X —Except—John 3:3.
Y oke—Matt. 11:29.
Z ealous—Tit. 2:14.

Other Alphabets.—The principle just explained can be applied indefinitely. Thus the name of one's city may be taken and a set of verses chosen from the Bible, one verse for each letter of the city's name. Thus:

B e of good cheer.
    Mark 14:27.
O ffend.
    In many things we offend all . . Jas. 3:2.
S pirit.
    God is a spirit. . . . John 4:24.
T ree. The tree is known by its fruit. . .
    Luke 6:44.
O vercometh.
    The victory that overcometh the world.
    . . . 1 John 5:4.
N oble.
    The Bereans were more noble. . . . Acts 17:11.

In this case the first letters of the key words spell the name, Boston.

The Juniors may learn a series of verses beginning with the letters of their own names, or of the name of the church, or of the pastor, to vary the bald alphabet rule.

"I Am" Verses.—Here is another series of verses that the Juniors may learn. The complete verses and not merely the phrases here given should be memorized.

I am that I am. Exod. 3:14.
I am the true vine. John 15:1.
I am the bread of life. John 6:20.
I am the light of the world. John 8:12.
I am the door. John 10:9.
I am the good shepherd. John 10:11.
I am the resurrection and the life. John 11:25.
I am the way, the truth, and the life. John 14:6.
I am he that liveth and was dead. Rev. 1:18.
I am alpha and omega. Rev. 1:8.

"I Will," or Words of Invitation.—Here are some fine verses to memorize; note the "I will" in each of them.

Invitation. Matt. 11:28-30.
Reception. John 6:37.
Healing. Matt. 8:2, 3.

Confession. Matt. 10:32.
Service. Matt. 4:19.
Comfort. John 14:18.
Subjection. Matt. 26:39.
Glorification. John 17:24.

More "I Will" Verses.—These verses are from the Psalms. The names we have given them suggest the lesson. Of course the list may be indefinitely extended.

I will trust. Ps. 4:8.
I will testify. Ps. 22:22.
I will teach. Ps. 51:13.
I will pray. Ps. 28:1.
I will obey. Ps. 119:32.
I will praise. Ps. 13:6.

Symbols-of-the-Spirit Verses. — The superintendent will explain the meaning of the symbols to the Juniors as they learn these verses.

Wind. John 3:8.
Oil. 1 John 2:20. (Compare the vision of the golden candlestick and the two olive trees in Zach. 4.)
Dove. John 1:32.
Rivers of Water. John 7:38, 39.
Tongues of Fire. Acts 2:3.

Memory Work in Connection with Great Topics.
—Often the daily readings given in the booklet, "The Daily Portion," contain verses that the Juniors may memorize, one verse a day, throughout the week. Sometimes the superintendent may make up a set of seven memory verses in connection with the topic for the following week and ask the Juniors to memorize them. The following is a suggestion taken from the great theme, "Salvation." Thus:

The purpose of salvation is
Godward—obedience. 1 Pet. 1:14.
Christward—fellowship or companionship with Him. 1 John 1:3.
Spiritward—filled with Him. Eph. 5:18.
Toward Others—loving service. 1 John 3:17.
Toward the World—be unlike it. Rom. 12:1, 2.
Toward Satan—overcome him. 1 John 2:14.
Toward Ourselves—self-denial. Luke 9:23.

Here Is Another Exercise on "God's Gifts."—
Good and perfect gifts. Jas. 1:17.
Eternal life. John 10:28.
Rest. Matt. 11:28.
Peace. John 14:27.
Salvation. Eph. 2:8.
All things. 1 Tim. 6:17.
A crown of life. Jas. 1:12.

BIBLE DRILLS—MEMORY WORK 161

Practical Passages.

OLD TESTAMENT MEMORY WORK.

1. Creation. Gen. 1:1-5.
2. The Ten Commandments. Exod. 20:3-17.
3. Benediction. Num. 6:24-26.
4. Memories. Deut. 8:2-5.
5. Two Men. Ps. 1:1-6.
6. The King. Ps. 2:1-12.
7. God's Greatness. Ps. 8:1-9.
8. God's Law. Ps. 19:7-14.
9. The Shepherd. Ps. 23:1-6.
10. Trust in God. Ps. 91:1-16.
11. Thanksgiving. Ps. 103:1-13.
12. Song of the Traveller. Ps. 121:1-8.
13. The House of God. Ps. 84:1-4, 10-12.

Practical Passages.

NEW TESTAMENT MEMORY WORK.

1. The Beatitudes. Matt. 5:3-12.
2. Sincerity. Matt. 5:33-37.
3. Christian Love. Matt. 5:38-48.
4. The Lord's Prayer. Matt. 6:9-13.
5. Anxiety. Matt. 6:25-34.
6. Unkind Words. Matt. 7:1-5.
7. Two Houses. Matt. 7:24-27.
8. Rest. Matt. 11:28-30.

9. Angels' Song. Luke 2:8-14.
10. The Lost Son. Luke 15:11-24.
11. Forgiveness. Luke 17:3, 4.
12. The True Light. John 1:1-14.
13. God's Love. John 3:14-17.
14. Life and Service. Rom. 12:1-21.
15. Paul's Hymn to Love. 1 Cor. 13:1-13.
16. Things to Think Over. Phil. 4:8.
17. Risen with Christ. Col. 3:1-4.
18. Sin and Pardon. 1 John 1:8-10; 2:1, 2.
19. The Father's Love. 1 John 3:1-3.
20. How to Love. 1 John 3:16-18.
21. The Song of Mary. Luke 1:46-55.
22. A Vision of the Redeemed. Rev. 7:13-17.
23. A Vision of Heaven. Rev. 22:1-5.
24. Diligent in Goodness. 2 Pet. 1:5-11.

A Bible-Biography Alphabet.

Juniors may be taught the stories of the men and women in the following list. Note that the first names spell out the entire alphabet, with the exception of W, Y, and X. This list does not by any means exhaust the possibilities of this method of creating interest in Bible biographies. For instance, for the letter "A" the name of Abraham has been selected. But there are others whose names begin with "A"—Ananias, for instance, or Annas, the high priest, or Aaron, the priest, the brother of Moses. The same thing is true of most

BIBLE DRILLS—MEMORY WORK

of the other letters, so that a live superintendent will follow this exercise with another biographical alphabet of her own. We are interested at present merely in presenting the method.

The life stories of these characters should be searched out and found as far as possible. We have given a single text as a starting point. A memory verse has been linked on to each character; but the Juniors should learn the whole story and not this one verse. These stories should be told in the meeting from time to time:

A is for Abraham. Gen. 12:1. Memory verse: Heb. 11:8.
B is for Balaam. Num. 22:5. Memory verse: Num. 22:34.
C is for Cain. Gen. 4:8. Memory verse: 1 John 3:12.
D is for David. 1 Sam. 16:8. Memory verse: Acts 13:36, 37.
E is for Elijah. 1 Kings 17:1. Memory verse: Jas. 5:17.
F is for Felix. Acts 24:10. Memory verse: Acts 24:25.
G is for Gideon. Judg. 6:11. Memory verse: Judg. 7:7.
H is for Hannah. 1 Sam. 1:11. Memory verse: 1 Sam. 2:2.
I is for Isaac. Gen. 22:2. Memory verse: Gen. 22:7.

J is for Jacob. Gen. 25:33, 34. Memory verse: Gen. 32:26.

K is for Korah. Num. 16:1. Memory verse: Jude 11.

L is for Lazarus. John 11:1. Memory verse John 11:25.

M is for Mary. Matt. 1:16. Memory verse: John 2:5.

N is for Noah. Gen. 6:8. Memory verse: Gen. 8:21.

O is for Onesimus. Philemon 10. Memory verse: Philemon 7.

P is for Peter. Matt. 4:18. Memory verse: Matt. 16:18.

Q is for Quartus. Rom. 16:23. Memory verse: Rom. 16:19.

R is for Ruth. Ruth 1:4. Memory verse: Ruth 1:16.

S is for Saul. 1 Sam. 9:2. Memory verse: 1 Sam. 15:23.

T is for Thomas. Matt. 10:3. Memory verse: John 4:5, 6.

U is for Uzza. 1 Chron. 13:7-10. Memory verse: John 2:16.

V is for Vashti. Esth. 1:9. Memory verse: 1 Tim. 2:9.

Z is for Zacchaeus. Luke 19:2. Memory verse: John 12:21.

Rewards.—Juniors crave recognition, and they should be rewarded suitably for good work done. Thus, a symbol such as a sun, a cross, a shield, and such like, should be prepared for each of the "Practical Passages" series of verses, and when a Junior learns one of the passages the appropriate symbol should be given him. These symbols should be strung on colored ribbons and kept in the society, the Juniors' names being written on a special card. The Juniors will watch these symbols increase in number and will work hard to get the next one. Symbols may be obtained from the United Society of Christian Endeavor, Boston, Mass.

For other memory work stars should be given to be fixed on the sashes of the Juniors. When a Junior has won five stars they should be exchanged for one crescent, and when he has won five crescents they should be changed for one sun. Or, if desired, the Juniors may be allowed to keep the stars and get a crescent in addition; and so with the crescents and suns.

An honor-roll may also be kept with stars of different colors placed opposite the names of the Juniors according to the memory work they have done.

Some societies give the Juniors special titles. The title "Page" is given to those that have studied "The Junior Text-Book." The title

"Squire" is earned by doing specific memory work and holding office or doing committee work. Those that reach a certain standard of memory work are called "Knights," while the title of "Royal Knight" is given to those that have earned all the other titles and are recommended by the pastor for faithfulness, character, growth, and service.

QUESTIONS FOR REVIEW

What is the value of Bible drills for Juniors?
How should we teach Juniors the names of Bible books?
Outline the relation of the Bible books to one another.
What is a verse-finding drill, and how conduct it?
What is the value of a spelling drill?
What is a Bible-biography drill?
How may we conduct a parable drill?
A map drill?
How are Bible alphabets made?
What is a Great Word alphabet?
Name some other alphabets.
Quote some "I Am" verses.
How may we use great topics in memory work?
Why should Juniors memorize great Bible passages?
What is a Bible-biography alphabet?
Why use honor-rolls in memory work?

CHAPTER XIII

SHORT BIBLE PRAYERS.

These prayers may be given to Juniors to memorize and use in the meeting as sentence prayers. The superintendent will find many Bible phrases, expressing supplication and aspiration, that are suitable for such prayers. The Psalms are especially rich in them. The texts may be written in full on cards—the prayer-meeting committee doing the work at home—or the references alone may be written. These cards the superintendent will give to Juniors whom she wishes to take part in the meeting in this way.

Supplication.

Ps. 17:5: Hold up my goings in my paths, that my footsteps slip not.

Ps. 17:8: Keep me as the apple of thine eye, hide me under the shadow of thy wings.

Mark 9:24: Lord I believe; help thou mine unbelief.

Luke 18:13: God be merciful to me a sinner.

Ps. 90:14: O satisfy us early with thy mercy; that we may rejoice and be glad all our days.

Ps. 90:17: Let the beauty of the Lord our God be upon us; and establish thou the work of our hands upon us; yea, the work of our hands establish thou it.

Ps. 51:1: Wash me thoroughly from mine iniquity, and cleanse me from my sin.

Aspiration.

Job 23:3: O that I knew where I might find him! that I might come even unto his seat!

Ps. 17:15: Hold up my goings in thy paths, that my footsteps slip not.

Ps. 18:1: I will love thee, O Lord, my strength.

Ps. 22:19: But be not thou far from me, O Lord; O my strength, haste thee to help me.

Ps. 25:4: Show me thy ways, O Lord; teach me thy path.

Ps. 26:8: Lord, I have loved the habitation of thy house, and the place where thine honor dwelleth.

Ps. 27:4: One thing have I desired of the Lord, that will I seek after: that I may dwell in the house of the Lord all the days of my life, to behold the beauty of the Lord, and to inquire in his temple.

1 Cor. 2:9: Eye hath not seen, nor ear heard, neither have entered into the heart of man, the things that God hath prepared for them that love him.

Ps. 84:1,2: O how amiable are thy tabernacles, O Lord of hosts! My soul longeth, yea, even fainteth, for the courts of the Lord; my heart and my flesh crieth out for the living God.

Eph. 3:14-19: For this cause I bow my knees unto the Father of our Lord Jesus Christ, of whom the whole family in heaven and earth is named; that he would grant you, according to the riches of his glory, to be strengthened with might by his Spirit in the inner man; that Christ may dwell in your hearts by faith; that ye, being rooted and grounded in love, may be able to comprehend with all saints what is the breadth, and length, and depth, and height; and to know the love of Christ, which passeth knowledge, that ye might be filled with all the fulness of God.

Praise.

Ps. 8:1: O Lord our God, how excellent is thy name in all the earth! who hast set thy glory above the heavens!

Ps. 9:1: I will praise thee, O Lord, with my whole heart; I will show forth thy marvellous works.

Ps. 18:30: As for God, his way is perfect; the word of the Lord is tried; he is a buckler to all those that trust in him.

Ps. 19:1: The heavens declare the glory of God; and the firmament declareth his handiwork.

Ps. 30:5: For his anger endureth but a moment: in his favor is life; weeping may endure for a night, but joy cometh in the morning.

Ps. 32:1: Blessed is he whose transgression is forgiven, whose sin is covered.

Ps. 32:2: Blessed is the man unto whom the Lord imputeth not iniquity, and in whose spirit there is no guile.

Ps. 34:4: I sought the Lord, and he heard me, and delivered me from all my fears.

Ps. 34:8: O taste and see that the Lord is good: blessed is the man that trusteth in him.

Faith.

Ps. 3:6: I will not be afraid of ten thousands of people, that have set themselves against me round about.

Ps. 5:3: My voice shalt thou hear in the morning, O Lord; in the morning will I direct my prayer unto thee, and will look up.

Ps. 5:11: But let all those that put their trust in thee rejoice: let them shout for joy, because thou defendest them; let them also that love thy name be joyful in thee.

Ps. 16:8: I have set the Lord always before me: because he is at my right hand, I shall not be moved.

Ps. 20:1: The Lord hear thee in the day of trouble; the name of the God of Jacob defend thee.

Ps. 23:1: The Lord is my shepherd, I shall not want.

Ps. 25:14: The secret of the Lord is with them that fear him; and he will show them his covenant.

Ps. 27:1: The Lord is my light and my salvation; whom shall I fear? The Lord is the strength of my life; of whom shall I be afraid?

Thanksgiving.

Exod. 15:2: The Lord is my strength and song, and he is become my salvation.

Ps. 18:35: Thou hast also given me the shield of thy salvation; and thy right hand hath holden me up, and thy gentleness hath made me great.

2 Cor. 9:15: Thanks be unto God for his unspeakable gift.

Ps. 103:1-5: Bless the Lord, O my soul; and all that is within me, bless his holy name. Bless the Lord, O my soul, and forget not all his benefits:

Who forgiveth all thine iniquities; who healeth all thy diseases; who redeemeth thy life from destruction; who crowneth thee with loving kindness and tender mercies; who satisfied thy mouth with good things, so that thy youth is renewed like the eagle's.

Ps. 100:1: Make a joyful noise unto the Lord, all ye lands.

Ps. 105:1, 2: O give thanks unto the Lord; call upon his name; make known his deeds among the people. Sing unto him, sing psalms unto him; talk ye of all his wondrous works.

Dedication.

Isa. 6:8: Here am I, send me.

Rom. 1:15: As much as in me is, I am ready.

1 Cor. 2:2: For I determined not to know anything among you but Jesus Christ and him crucified.

Benedictions.

Num. 6:24-26: The Lord bless thee and keep thee; the Lord make his face to shine upon thee and be gracious unto thee; the Lord lift up his countenance upon thee, and give thee peace.

Rom. 11:33: O the depth of the riches both of the wisdom and knowledge of God! How unsearchable are his judgments, and his ways past finding out!

1 Thess. 5:23: And the very God of peace sanctify you wholly; and I pray God your whole spirit and soul and body may be preserved blameless unto the coming of our Lord Jesus Christ.

2 Thess. 3:16: Now the God of peace himself give you peace always by all means. The Lord be with you all.

Rom. 8:38, 39: For I am persuaded that neither death, nor life, nor angels, nor principalities, nor powers, nor things present, nor things to come, nor height, nor depth, nor any other creature, shall be able to separate us from the love of God, which is in Christ Jesus our Lord.

1 Cor. 15:57, 58: But thanks be to God which giveth us the victory through our Lord Jesus Christ. Therefore, my beloved brethren, be ye steadfast, unmovable, always abounding in the work of the Lord, forasmuch as ye know that your labor is not in vain in the Lord.

2 Cor. 13:14: The grace of the Lord Jesus Christ, and the love of God, and the communion of the Holy Ghost, be with you all.

Heb. 13:20, 21: Now the God of peace, that brought again from the dead our Lord Jesus, that great shepherd of the sheep, through the blood of the everlasting covenant, make you perfect in every good work to do his will, working in you that which is well pleasing in his sight, through Jesus Christ; to whom be glory for ever and ever.

1 John 5:20: And we know that the Son of God is come, and hath given us an understanding, that we may know him that is true; and we are in him that is true, even in his Son Jesus Christ. This is the true God and eternal life.

Rev. 1:5, 6: Unto him that loved us, and washed us from our sins in his own blood, and hath made us kings and priests unto God and his Father; to him be glory and dominion for ever and ever.

Jude 24: Now unto him that is able to keep you from

falling, and to present you faultless before the presence of his glory with exceeding joy; to the only wise, God our Saviour, be glory and majesty, dominion and power, both now and ever.

1 Tim. 1:17: Now to the King eternal, immortal, invisible, the only wise God, be honor and glory for ever and ever.

Eph. 3:20: Now unto him that is able to do exceeding abundantly above all that we ask or think, according to the power that worketh in us, unto him be glory in the church by Jesus Christ throughout all ages, world without end.

Using the Bible in Prayer.—The superintendent may also teach the Juniors how to use the Bible in their prayers, quoting Bible words that express their ideas. Thus a Junior may pray:

"Lord; help me to cast all my care on thee, for thou carest for me." The *thought*, but not necessarily the exact words is given. An example or two may be helpful, but the superintendent will easily find others for herself.

"O Lord, may we feel that we are lights in the world and seek to shine for thee."

"Make us pure in heart, dear Father, for it is the pure in heart that see God."

"Keep us from being quarrelsome, O Lord, because it is the peacemaker that is a child of God."

"We thank thee that thou didst so love the world that thou didst give thy Son for us, to save us from sin and death."

"Lord, we would believe in thee; help thou our unbelief and weakness."

"We would be taught by thee, Lord Jesus, so that we may grow more like thee day by day."

Some Sentence Prayers.—The following prayers are suggestions only. Use them with Juniors to give the children an idea of what a sentence prayer should be.

"Lord Jesus, make this day a blessing to me, and make me a blessing to others."

"Thou hast promised never to forsake me, O Lord, therefore I will be brave and strong."

"Help us to forget ourselves and pity others who are in trouble."

"Forgive us, Lord Jesus, if we have neglected our duty, and help us to do better in future."

"Thou hast promised not to send us away empty, O Lord, therefore may we be blest to-day."

"The thanksgiving we would offer thee, Lord Jesus, is to live according to thy will and love thee."

"We open our hearts to thee, dear Lord, enter thou and make us thine."

The superintendent should teach the Juniors to use the different names of Jesus and of God in prayer. Many always use the same expression, "Dear Jesus," or something like that. Make for variety: "Lord Jesus," "O Lord," "O Christ," "Our Saviour," and so on.

SHORT BIBLE PRAYERS

QUESTIONS FOR REVIEW

How may we use short Bible prayers for sentence prayers?
What kind of Bible prayers are suitable for Juniors to use?
Where in the Bible may superintendents find such prayers?
Write out three Bible benedictions.
How may we use Bible ideas in our prayers?
Why should Juniors be taught to vary the titles of God and Jesus in prayer?

CHAPTER XIV

A FEW SUGGESTIONS

In this chapter we propose to gather up some practical suggestions that superintendents may find useful.

Sashes, Stars, Crescents, and Suns.—Bright colors, the spectacular, anything distinctive, appeal to Juniors. Therefore many societies have sashes or regalia which the children wear in the meeting. They are kept in the meeting room, and usually a Junior has charge of handing them out in the meeting, gathering them together after the meeting is over, and folding them neatly and putting them away. The United Society sells sashes of taffeta ribbon for this purpose, but superintendents may make their own sashes if they desire. The sashes should be worn diagonally across the chest.

Officers are given red sashes, committee chairmen get blue sashes, and the rest of the members get white sashes.

Stars, crescents, and suns may also be used and pinned on the sashes in recognition of memory

A FEW SUGGESTIONS 177

and other work done by the Juniors. Societies that use the Junior Training Chart will find their instructions as to the use of these symbols in carrying out the programme suggested on the chart.

Parents and the Pledge.—It will repay the superintendent if she or an associate can visit the parents of the Juniors who are proposed for membership in the society. She should take with her a copy of the Junior Pledge, show it to the child's mother, and explain it to her. In a tactful way the co-operation of parents should be asked to see that the children as far as possible are encouraged to do their best to keep the pledge. A child's home produces a profound impression on its mind. If the home is right, the child has a much better chance of turning out well than if the home is a place of indifference to religion or a place of strife. Christian parents will no doubt do what they can to help the child; and even non-Christian parents, for the child's sake, may try to encourage it.

Mothers' Meetings. — Hold occasionally a mothers' meeting, the mothers of the children being invited to come. This is not a meeting of the society; the children are not to be present. The idea is to interest the mothers and win their co-operation. The superintendent may act as a kind of conference leader, after refreshments have been served, and deal with the question how best to help the children. Talks by expert Junior workers should be arranged. In many places the mothers of the Juniors will promise to assist in every way they can, by getting the Juniors to attend on time, by reminding them of their duties, by encouraging them, and by trying to interest also non-Christian mothers.

Perhaps at first only a few mothers will come to such a meeting. They may be formed into a committee to go after the others and hold a second meeting with a larger attendance. If the home can be made to work with the society the superintendent's hands will be immensely strengthened.

Then, of course, the mothers may be invited occasionally to visit the society and see how the work is done. To many it will be a revelation, for they do not realize what Junior Christian Endeavor means.

In the same way the fathers should be invited to another meeting, and this meeting the boys of the society should conduct, although the girls will also take part.

Banners.—Every live Junior society will want a banner. If there is money enough in the treasury a beautiful banner of silk may be bought.

A FEW SUGGESTIONS 179

If not, deft-fingered Junior girls may make a banner out of cheaper material.

Take a pattern of the shape and size from some banner you have seen. Then cut a piece of flannel or other cloth the proper size. If you can afford to cover this with silk, you will have a fine banner; but if not, a very good banner may be made by covering the cloth with lustred paper. White paper makes a beautiful background on which red, blue and gold letters may be pasted. The letters will have to be carefully drawn and cut out of colored paper.

What should the banner contain? If it is big enough it should contain the Christian Endeavor motto, "For Christ and the Church." At all events it should have the word "Junior," and the monogram, "C. E." Many banners contain also the name of the society. Fancy tassels worked with the Junior colors, blue and white, may be made from thread or yarn.

In these days the staff and cross bar will not be difficult to obtain. They may be painted white.

For carrying in processions or at picnics, or for decorating the meeting room, blue felt pennants may be used with the Christian Endeavor monogram in white.

If the Juniors do handwork, they should make armbands of blue cloth with the Christian Endeavor monogram in white sewed on them. If cloth cannot be obtained then make the armbands of paper. These may be worn at parades, at Christian Endeavor rallies, and so on.

Buttons and Pins.—Celluloid buttons are cheap and they can be used as rewards for Junior work well done. When a Junior has earned so many buttons, he may exchange them for a Christian Endeavor pin. Every Junior should be encouraged to wear the Christian Endeavor monogram in some form or other, on a button or a pin. Make this a point in some of the contests the society carries out.

QUESTIONS FOR REVIEW

How may we use sashes, crescents, and suns in the society?
How may parents help Juniors to keep the pledge?
How may we secure the co-operation of parents?
Why hold mothers' meetings?
Why use banners, and how make them?
What use can be made of buttons and pins in Junior work?

CHAPTER XV

JUNIOR UNIONS

The Junior Union has a twofold character. It is first a union of superintendents, and second a union of Juniors. And since the union of Juniors needs adult supervision, which naturally comes from the superintendents, the two parts must be so organized as to co-operate harmoniously.

The Superintendents.—It is advisable that all the Junior superintendents in a city or district get together and organize a union of superintendents. This union should meet once a month or so, and the purpose of the union will be to discuss problems of Junior work, exchange plans of working, relate experiences, listen to talks by Junior expert workers, exhibit Junior handwork, and in every way work for the efficiency of the superintendents and the improvement of the societies.

The union should have officers, president, treasurer, and secretary. It may have committees too (if the union is small probably there will not be more than one person on each committee), especially a lookout committee to study the possibilities of organizing new societies. This will be a special part of the union's work, and in it all the members should take part. They should make a survey of the churches of the district and if there are any that have no Junior society, they should approach the pastor with a proposal to start one. They may arrange to take groups of Juniors to the church and hold a model meeting.

Round Robins.—The superintendents may reach into the wider field and gather experience for their work. The State Junior superintendent may start a Round Robin, first ascertaining from all the superintendents in the State whether or not they wish to participate. This Round Robin will contain a list of the names of superintendents to whom it should be sent; brief instructions; and each superintendent who receives it may keep it a day or two, take notes of helpful plans, insert suggestions and plans of her own, and send it on its way to the next name on the list.

The Junior Union.—This will be modelled on the Senior Union, but modified to suit the limitations nature has imposed on Juniors. Juniors may be elected to the offices of president, secretary, and treasurer; but to each office an adult

JUNIOR UNIONS

supervisor should also be attached. Thus one superintendent will be appointed to advise the Junior president; another to advise the treasurer; and a third to advise the secretary and see that the work is properly done.

The principal object of the union will be to hold rallies and conventionettes and to organize the Junior section of the Senior rallies, when such sections are planned. It need hardly be pointed out that the Juniors in this way will get invaluable training for the larger work of Christian Endeavor.

Perhaps the only practical committee for a Junior Union will be the flower committee, which will help to decorate the churches where rallies are to be held.

The Junior executive committee will meet with the advisers and make out a programme for the rally. In the rally the Junior president will preside, his adviser sitting beside him to help him when help is needed. The Junior secretary will call the roll.

The Juniors should be given a large part on the programme. There may be an adult speaker, perhaps, but not one that will make a long-winded and dry speech. At the rallies there will be special Bible drills put on by single societies; united Bible drills, such as finding Bible verses, repeating texts of Scripture; and short essays or talks by Juniors on various aspects of Christian Endeavor work.

In the conventionette, which usually will be held on a Saturday afternoon, Junior conferences should be held under adult leadership. They will deal with the work of the various committees. All members of the prayer meeting committee, for instance, will meet in the prayer-meeting conference and discuss plans to make better prayer meetings. And so with the other committees.

The Junior Parade.—When a rally is to be held, or a conventionette, Juniors will advertise their societies well if they hold a Junior parade. This may of course be held also at rallies and conventions of Senior societies.

The best plan is to have all the Juniors of the city meet at a given church some distance from the convention church. Arrange the Juniors by societies, a Junior at the head of each carrying the society banner with the name of the society. Some may be more ambitious and make a large banner to be carried by two staffs, one at each side, the banner between them. This will bear the name of the society and also a sentence or two telling about Junior work. All Juniors should wear white armbands with the Christian Endeavor monogram in blue. As many as possible may carry pennants—make them of blue paper with the Christian Endeavor monogram in white, if you have not cloth ones.

Many unions might well organize a Junior band which could march at the head of the parade.

Of course all the superintendents and assistants will be present to keep order. The route should be carefully planned by the superintendents beforehand, and a number of members of the Senior societies should be enlisted to come to the parade to take care of the Juniors.

Automobile Parade.—Something that will create an even deeper impression on the public and at the same time arouse the enthusiasm of every Junior would be an automobile parade. The members of the churches will lend their automobiles for this purpose, and a good many Juniors may be carried in each auto. There would be pennants and banners in this case too, and big streamers on the automobiles would announce the meaning of the parade.

The Junior Union Treasury.—The expenses of a Junior union will not be heavy, but there will be posters to get out, announcements of the meeting to mail, car-fare of speakers to provide for, and such matters. The ideal way to provide funds for this is to apportion the annual budget among the societies. It will be the duty of the treasurer to get this money and to disburse it, directed by his or her adviser.

When the State has a Junior department with a superintendent of Junior work it is an excellent plan to add to the budget and apportion a small amount so that the union as such may send a gift to the State work. This applies also to county work if there is such in the county.

We believe it is advisable for States to keep Junior contributions distinct from other gifts. It often happens at State and other conventions, that a Senior society will make a pledge to State work, and then count toward their pledge whatever the Junior society gives. The Junior gift is lost in the larger gift. The Senior society should pledge for itself, and the Junior for itself, each making good its own obligation.

The State union should plan to use Junior gifts for the spread of Junior work. It will get more money if this is done, for the Juniors will easily take to such missionary enterprise and will give more liberally toward it.

The Junior Union Secretary.—The secretary and adviser will keep a record of societies, number of members, names of superintendent, president, and secretary as well as their addresses.

JUNIOR UNIONS

The secretary will send these names to the offices of the county and State unions.

She will also keep minutes of executive committee meetings and of all rallies. A copy of the programme used at each rally should be written into the report, although it need not be read when the minutes are read. It will be there for the information of later officers who may want to know how previous meetings were planned and conducted.

QUESTIONS FOR REVIEW

What is the twofold character of a Junior union?
How organize a union of superintendents?
What is the value of a superintendents' union?
What is a Round Robin?
What is a Junior union and how is it organized?
What may a Junior union's officers do at a Junior rally?
What is a Junior conventionette?
What is the value of Junior parades, and how arrange them?
Why keep Junior funds for union work separate from the union's funds derived from other sources?
What is the work of the Junior union secretary?

www.ingramcontent.com/pod-product-compliance
Lightning Source LLC
Chambersburg PA
CBHW031352040426
42444CB00005B/253